The Homebrewed Christianity
Guide to the Old Testament

The Homebrewed Christianity Guide to the Old Testament

Israel's In-Your-Face, Holy God

ROLF A. JACOBSON
AUTHOR

TRIPP FULLER
SERIES EDITOR

Fortress Press
Minneapolis

THE HOMEBREWED CHRISTIANITY GUIDE TO
THE OLD TESTAMENT
Israel's In-Your-Face, Holy God

Cover Design: Jesse Turri
Book Design and Typesetting: PerfecType, Nashville, TN

Print ISBN: 978-1-5064-0635-0
eBook ISBN: 978-1-5064-0636-7

The paper used in this publication meets the minimum
requirements of American National Standard for Information Sciences — Permanence of Paper for Printed Library
Materials, ANSI Z329.48-1984.

Manufactured in the U.S.A.

For Karl
brother, best of friends, faithful and formidable scholar

Contents

Series Introduction

You are about to read a guidebook. Not only is the book the sweet "guidebook" size, shaped perfectly to take a ride in your back pocket, but the book itself was crafted with care by a real-deal theology nerd. Here's the thing. The Homebrewed Christianity Guide series has one real goal: we want to think *with* you, not *for* you.

The whole "homebrew" metaphor grows from my passion for helping anyone who wants to geek out about theology to do so with the best ingredients around. That's why I started the Homebrewed Christianity podcast in 2008, and that's why I am thrilled to partner with Fortress Press's Theology for the People team to produce this series. I am confident that the church has plenty of intelligent and passionate people who want a more robust conversation about their faith.

A podcast, in case you're wondering, is like talk radio on demand without the commercials. You download a file and listen when, if, where, and how long you want. I love the podcast medium. Short of talking one-on-one, there's hardly a more intimate presence than speaking to someone in their earbuds as they're stuck in traffic, on the treadmill, or washing dishes. When I started the podcast,

I wanted to give anyone the option of listening to some of the best thinkers from the church and the academy.

Originally, the podcast was for friends, family, and my local pub theology group. I figured people in the group were more likely to listen to a podcast than read a giant book. So as the resident theology nerd, I read the books and then interviewed the authors. Soon, thousands of people were listening. Since then the audience has grown to over fifty thousand unique listeners each month and over a million downloads. A community of listeners, whom we call Deacons, grew, and we've got a cast of cohosts and regular guests.

Over the better part of a decade, I have talked to scores of theologians and engaged with the Deacons about these conversations. It has been a real joy. Every time I hear from a listener, I do the happy dance in my soul.

And here's the deal: I love theology, but I love the church more. I am convinced that the church can really make a difference in the world. But in order to do that, it needs to face reality rather than run from it. The church must use its brain, live its faith, and join God in working for the salvation of the world. And that's what these books are all about.

We often open and close the podcast by reminding listeners that we are providing the ingredients so that they can brew their own faith. That's the same with these books. Each author is an expert theological brewer, and they've been asked to write from their own point of view. These guidebooks are not boringly neutral; instead, they are zestily provocative, meant to get you thinking and brewing.

I look forward to hearing from you on the Speakpipe at HomebrewedChristianity.com and meeting you at an HBC 3D event. We can drink a pint and talk about this book, how you agree and disagree with it. Because if we're talking about theology, the world is a better place.

And remember: Share the Brew!

Tripp Fuller

The Homebrewed Posse

Whether it's the podcast, the blog, or live events, Homebrewed Christianity has always been a conversation, and these books are no different. So inside of this and every volume in the HBC book series, you'll be hearing from four members of the Homebrewed community. They are:

THE BISHOP

The Bishop: Kindly, pastoral, encouraging. She's been around the block a few times, and nothing ruffles her feathers. She wants everyone to succeed, and she's an optimist, so she knows they will.

THE ELDER

The Elder: Scolding, arrogant, know-it-all. He's old and disgruntled, the father figure you can never please. He loves quoting doctrine; he's the kind of guy who controls every church meeting because he knows Roberts Rules of Order better than anyone else.

THE DEACON

The Deacon: Earnest, excited, energetic. He's a guy who has just discovered HBC, and he can't get enough of it. He's a cheerleader, a shouter, an encourager. He's still in his first naïveté.

THE ACOLYTE

The Acolyte: Smart, inquisitive, skeptical. She's the smartest student in your confirmation class. She's bound to be a biologist or a physicist, and she's skeptical of all the hocus pocus of Christianity. But she hasn't given up on it yet, so her questions come from the heart. She really wants to know if all this stuff works.

We look forward to continuing the conversation with you, online and in person!

Introduction

This volume focuses on the narrative arc of the Old Testament from Genesis through Ezra and Nehemiah. From the stories of creation through the stories of Israel's ancestors and their dealings with God, through the stories of Israel as a people and nation, through the stories of its exile in Babylon and inglorious return to a reduced land, it is the story of Israel's holy and in-your-face God. It is the story of God's faithfulness to the beloved creation and to the people God chose to be God's priestly people—a people through whom God could bless all the families of the earth and the earth itself. Along the way, we will also hear a little from Israel's greatest prophets—Amos, Hosea, Isaiah of Jerusalem, Micah, Jeremiah, Ezekiel, and Second Isaiah. At the end, there is a brief chapter on the Psalms—the heart of Israel's poetry of faith. Israel's way of getting back in the face of its in-your-face and holy God. The argument of this book is that Israel's wild-not-tame yet faithful-and-good God is both holy and faithful.

Throughout this book, I have opted to use my own translations from the biblical Hebrew—some are straight translations and others a bit more tongue-in-cheek paraphrases. I trust you can tell the difference. Unless otherwise noted, the translations are my own.

I am grateful to Tripp Fuller for the invitation to be part of the Homebrewed Christianity Guide series. It is an honor to be counted in the number with Tripp and the other authors and contributors to the series. I am very grateful to Tony Jones of Fortress Press for cajoling me to finish the project and for his strong editorial work. I love you, Tony.

I am honored to dedicate this book to my brother Karl N. Jacobson. An anonymous prophet strolled up to me and Karl at a Stevie Ray Vaughn concert in 1989. Looking back and forth between the two of us and taking in our obvious visual similarities and common genetic defects, he anointed my forehead with a greasy hand and said to both of us, "You ain't heavy man . . . you're brothers." It is wonderful to have a brother with whom I share so much. The love of God. Twin vocations as pastors and Old Testament scholars. Many friends and common passions for sports, games, literature, and food (although not for the same music—no friendship is perfect). And a deep love for each other as friend and brother. My life is better because I get to go through it with you. I thank God for you, Karl. You ain't heavy.

The Old Testament— The Library of an In-Your-Face God

The Old Testament's In-Your-Face God

The Old Testament is wild. Kind of like the God we meet in its pages. In C. S. Lewis's Narnia series, the Christ-figure Aslan is described as a wild-but-good lion. In *The Lion, the Witch, and the Wardrobe*, when Aslan is introduced, Mr. Beaver says, "Aslan is a lion—*the* Lion, the great Lion." "Ooh" Susan says. "I'd thought he was a man. Is he—quite safe? I shall feel rather nervous about meeting a lion." "Safe?" Mr. Beaver replies. "Who said anything about safe? 'Course he isn't safe. But he's good. He's the King, I tell you." Later, Mr. Beaver says, "Only

1

you mustn't press him. He's wild, you know. Not like a *tame* lion."[1]

In that description, Lewis aptly captures the nature of the God of the Bible—the God of both the Old Testament and New Testament. They are the same God after all, at least according to the Christian way of making sense of the Old Testament. God is wild. Not safe. Not tame. The king. The Old Testament itself is like that. Readers who try to tame the Old Testament—to stick its God in a cage or to neatly wrap up all of the loose ends—will either grow frustrated or be reduced to shrinking the Old Testament's three-dimensional witness to God and life to a flat, two-dimensional, photoshopped portrait.

THE BISHOP

It's easier to put God in a cage if you only preach on the Gospel texts.

Israel was not a creedal religion—a religion in which a statement of belief was recited in worship. But many times in the Old Testament, some version of the following creedal-like statement can be heard. In what may be one of the oldest passages in the Old Testament, the Lord passes in front of Moses and reveals the Lord's character:

> Moses cut two tablets of stone like the former ones [on which the Ten Commandments were written]. He arose early in the morning and went up on Mount Sinai, as the Lord had commanded

him, and took in his hand the two tablets of stone. The Lord descended in the cloud and stood with him there, and proclaimed the name, "The Lord." The Lord passed before him, and proclaimed,

The Lord, the Lord,
  a God merciful and gracious,
slow to anger, and abounding in faithful love
      and faithfulness,
keeping faithful love to the thousandth
      generation,
    forgiving iniquity and transgression and sin.
Yet by no means ignoring sin,
    but visiting the iniquity of the parents
upon the children and the children's children,
    to the third and the fourth generation.

So Moses quickly bowed his head toward the earth, and worshiped. He said, "If now I have found favor in your sight, O Lord, I pray, let the Lord go with us. Although this is a stiff-necked people, pardon our iniquity and our sin, and take us for your inheritance." (Exodus 34:4–9)

In this fragment, the Old Testament presents us with the core of its paradoxical witness to the character and activity of God. On the one hand, God is holy, with a finely tuned sense of justice and hatred of oppression. As such, God cannot abide sin—God's very holiness and the justice that dwells near the center of God's heart demands it. God will by no means ignore sin. Indeed, sometimes the sin of parents—like the dysfunctions of an alcoholic or abusive family system—will cascade down to the children, grand-children, and even great-grandchildren of the sinner. When God shows up, God's very voice hurts our ears, even when God whispers. The very sight of God pains you, like when a super bright light momentarily blinds you in a pitch-black room. The very touch of God makes you flinch like, well, when you flinch back from an electric spark.

THE ACOLYTE

I guess if you are gonna use masculine pronouns for God it can start with identifying the pain his mansplaining whisper can cause.

On the other hand, God is faithful, God is merciful, God is gracious, God abounds in faithful love and keeps promises *to the thousandth generation!* If justice is near the center of God's heart, mercy and fidelity are at the center of God's heart and character. At times, God's mercy and God's justice wage a closely fought battle in the heart of God. But in the end, mercy and faithfulness win. And while sin might be punished to the fourth generation, God's fidelity is kept to the thousandth generation. I am not great at math, but even I can see that that is quite a disparity.

The witness of the Old Testament is that the math works out in our favor. Even though we cannot serve the Lord adequately or faithfully. Even though we cannot love our neighbor perfectly. Even though we—the people of God—are a "stiff-necked people," God stays with us and is faithful to the divine promise. One thousand is still a lot more than four.

The answer isn't 42, but 996.

THE DEACON

More on that a little later. First, a little primer on what the Old Testament is (and isn't).

A Brief Overview of the Old Testament Library

The Old Testament is not really a book. More properly, the Old Testament is *books*—a library:

Books of stories. Books of poetry. Books of songs. Books of proverbs. Books of prophecy. Books of law. Books of wise sayings (and some foolish sayings). Books of legends. Books of history.

When it comes to counting, organizing, ordering, naming, and even understanding the various books of the Old Testament, there are various systems. Sort of a Dewey Decimal versus Library of Congress difference. Except here, it's also a matter of faith. Or faiths.

The Old Testament is the holy book (holy library) of both Judaism and Christianity. Judaism calls this holy library either the Jewish Bible or the Tanak. Christianity calls it the Old Testament (or sometimes the First Testament). Some academic scholars who study this library for a living call it the Hebrew Bible, because most of it was written in the ancient Hebrew language.[2]

There are actually multiple forms of Judaism—Reformed, Conservative, Orthodox, Hasidic, Secular. And there are multiple forms of Christianity—Roman Catholic, Orthodox (of various forms), Mainline Protestant, Evangelical Protestant. And while all Judaisms and all Protestant Christianities have the same books in the Old Testament/Jewish Bible, they organize them and order them differently. And the Roman Catholic and various Orthodox Christianities include extra books in their versions of the Old Testament. All of which can be "a very head-aching problem," as an old friend of mine once said.

So here's a brief guide.

Thumbnail Version

Jews organize their Bible into three major divisions, while Christians organize their Old Testament into five major divisions.

Judaism	Christianity
Torah (Hebrew: *Torah**)	Law
Prophets (*Nevi'im**)	History
Writings (*Ketuvim**)	Poetry (Wisdom)
	Major Prophets
	Minor Prophets

*Hence, the Jewish acronym "TaNaK" (Torah + Nevi'im + Ketuvim) for the Bible

The above charts only account for Jewish and Protestant systems of organizing and counting the books of the

I am having Vacation
Bible School flashbacks!!

THE ACOLYTE

Don't worry there are
ZERO pledges in this
book . . . no US flag,
Christian flag, or Bible
pledge.

THE DEACON

Old Testament. Roman Catholics and the various Eastern
Orthodox Churches include extra books in their Old Testament. These books are known to Protestants and Jews
as the Apocrypha.

All of these books were also written by the ancient
Israelite communities who wrote, collected, and curated
the library of holy books known as the Old Testament.
But the books included in the Apocrypha only survived
in Greek, not Hebrew. Some were probably written in
Hebrew but only survived in Greek. Others were probably
written directly in Greek. But through whatever process,
these books only survived in Greek, so that when the Jewish community came to the point of deciding which scrolls
would be included in the official canon, they rejected
all of the scrolls that were not in Hebrew. This decision
came after the split between Judaism and Christianity
had happened—by which point the larger pile of scrolls

Cheat-Sheet Version

Judaism	Christianity
Torah	*Law*
Genesis	Genesis
Exodus	Exodus
Leviticus	Leviticus
Numbers	Numbers
Deuteronomy	Deuteronomy
Prophets	*History*
Joshua	Joshua
Judges	Judges
1–2 Samuel	Ruth
1–2 Kings	1–2 Samuel
Isaiah	1–2 Kings
Jeremiah	1–2 Chronicles
Ezekiel	Ezra
Hosea	Nehemiah
Joel	Esther
Amos	*Poetry (Wisdom)*
Obadiah	Job
Jonah	Psalms
Micah	Proverbs
Nahum	Ecclesiastes
Habakkuk	Song of Songs
Zephaniah	*Major Prophets*
Haggai	Isaiah
Zechariah	Jeremiah
Malachi	Lamentations
Writings	Ezekiel
Psalms	Daniel
Proverbs	*Minor Prophets*
Job	Hosea
Song of Songs	Joel
Ruth	Amos
Lamentations	Obadiah
Ecclesiastes	Jonah
Esther	Micah
Daniel	Nahum
Ezra	Habakkuk
Nehemiah	Zephaniah
1–2 Chronicles	Haggai
	Zechariah
	Malachi

that included the Greek-only scrolls had already become accepted by the early, Greek-speaking Christian church. This is why early Rabbinic Judaism developed a different Bible than the early Christian church's Old Testament.

For the rest of the story, fast-forward to the year 1534, when Martin Luther—the first Protestant leader—was deciding which Old Testament canon to go with, the Jewish or the Catholic (or one of the Orthodox Church's canons). Luther chose to go with the Jewish canon, but he did include the apocryphal books in his German Bible of 1534. He said that these books were not Scripture, but they were "good and useful to read."

The books and additions to books that are included in the Roman Catholic Old Testament are:

- 1–2 Maccabees
- Sirach
- Tobit
- Judith
- Additions to Esther
- Wisdom (of Solomon)
- Baruch
- Additions to Daniel

Additional books and additions to books are included in the canons of various Orthodox Churches. But now we are getting really far down into the weeds. Time to pull up for some air.

The History of the Old Testament: A Very Brief Guide

The order of the books doesn't exactly help a person understand what the books are about. So for those readers who like to think in terms of a timeline, here is a brief guide.

Prehistory

Some portions of the Old Testament describe the creation of the world and other mythological stories about events before the advent of writing, human records, and human history. These stories include the creation of the world and the human race, the beginning of brokenness of the world, the flood story, and the beginnings of the diversity of human languages, ethnicity, and race.

Where in the Bible: Genesis 1–11; Job 38–41; Psalms 8, 19, 104, and 139; Proverbs 8–9.

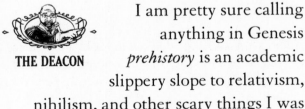

THE DEACON

I am pretty sure calling anything in Genesis *prehistory* is an academic slippery slope to relativism, nihilism, and other scary things I was warned about at Bible college.

Early History of Israel's Ancestors— Time Period: Before 1500 BCE

The Old Testament describes God's choice of one family and tribe—Abraham and Sarah's—to be a "priestly kingdom and holy nation" (Exodus 19:6) who will "be a blessing" and in whom "all the families of the earth shall be blessed" (Genesis 12:1–3). God promises this people a blessing, a land, and descendants who will become a great nation. These are the stories of Abraham and Sarah; Isaac and Rebekah; Jacob, Rachel, and Leah; Joseph and his brothers. Their story ends with the people living in Egypt.

Where in the Bible: Genesis 12–50; see also Psalms 78, 105, 106, and 136.

Exodus, Entry into the Land, and Time of the Judges— Time Period: ca. 1280–1040 BCE

After some centuries in Egypt, the people are enslaved by Pharaoh, the king of Egypt. God raises up Moses to free the people. At Mount Sinai, God enters into a holy, covenant relationship with the people and gives them the law, the center of which is the Ten Commandments. God brings the people into the promised land, where God serves directly as the people's Lord. The people live as twelve separate tribes until they demand a king "like all the other nations." Some people don't know how good they've got it!

Where in the Bible: Exodus, Leviticus, Numbers, Deuteronomy, Joshua, Judges, Ruth.

The United Monarchy—
Time Period: ca. 1040–922 BCE

For around one hundred years and three kings, Israel is one people, under God, indivisible, with ever diminishing liberty and justice for some. Israel demands a king, and God gives them what they want. Be careful what you pray for; God might give it to you! Israel's first king, Saul, is a hot mess who descends into mental illness. He's followed by David, who is remembered as Israel's greatest king by those people who never actually read about his cray-cray life in the actual Bible. After David, his son Solomon reigns. This period is often nostalgically viewed as a golden age in Israel's history because David fights wars and moves the capital to Jerusalem, where Solomon builds a magnificent temple and fortifies the kingdom. But David's wars followed by Solomon's building projects mean high taxes and a weary people. After Solomon's death, the northern tribes rebel against Jerusalem's regime. The northern ten tribes form the kingdom of Israel, and the southern tribes form the kingdom of Judah.

Where in the Bible: 1–2 Samuel, 1 Kings 1–11, 1 Chronicles, 2 Chronicles 1–9.

The Divided Monarchy—
Time Period: ca. 922–587 BCE

Following the split, the Northern Kingdom is the more populated, prosperous, and powerful. Founded by a king named Rehoboam, it is ruled over two centuries by a series of short-lived dynasties. Its capital is Samaria (whence its descendants later take the name *Samaritans*). The nation worships the Lord but also goes astray by worshiping other gods, such as the fertility gods Baal and Asherah. In addition, gross injustice and violations of the Lord's commandments are the rule of the day. A series of important prophets appear and call the people back to faithfulness—Elijah, Elisha, Micaiah, Hosea, and Amos. Toward the end of its span, the kings of Israel are forced to submit to the empire of Assyria. After a series of rebellions against Assyria, the northern kingdom of Israel is destroyed and much of its people are forced into exile in 722 BCE. Many of these people become the "lost tribes of Israel" and disappear into the mists of history—losing their identity and their faith in exile. Much of the populace also remains in the land, and some flee south and join the kingdom of Judah.

The southern kingdom of Judah, in spite of being smaller and weaker, has three great advantages: a consistent line of David's descendants as its kings, the capital city of Jerusalem, and the spiritual center of the people in the temple on Mount Zion. Injustice, idolatry, and political weakness threaten the health and survival of the people. God sends a series of important prophets to call the people to faithfulness—Isaiah, Micah, Jeremiah, Habakkuk, Nahum, and more. Judah survives the attacks of the Assyrian empire and lasts longer than Israel. In the end, however, it meets a similar fate—this time at the hands of the Babylonian Empire. In 597 BCE, the Babylonians force Jerusalem to surrender and deport a portion of the populace into exile in Babylon. When Judah's last king rebels again, the Babylonian army completely destroys Jerusalem in 587 and deports a second wave of its populace into exile. For all appearances, the history of God's experiment with Israel seems at an end.

Where in the Bible: 1 Kings 12–22; 2 Kings; 2 Chronicles 10–36; Isaiah 1–39; Micah; Jeremiah; Habakkuk; Nahum; Zephaniah; Jonah.

The Exile and the Diaspora— Time Period: 597/587–539 BCE

Following the first deportation (597) and the second deportation and destruction of Jerusalem (587), a miraculous thing happens—even though they have been sent into exile, the people survive. Their prophets preach hope—especially Jeremiah, Ezekiel, and an anonymous prophet known as Second Isaiah. Scribes keep busy copying and preserving Israel's Scriptures—the Torah, the prophets, many psalms, and Israel's history. And not only do the people survive, but they maintain their identity as God's people.

Just as noteworthy are the changes that take place among God's people. First, they switch from being a holy nation living in a holy land to being a holy people living throughout the world. The people scatter across the ancient landscape—some go into exile, some stay in the land, and others go to Egypt, to Syria, to Asia Minor, and further. This scattering is called the *diaspora*. The people also start to become a people of the holy book (the origins of the Old Testament). And in 539, when Cyrus of Persia conquers Babylon, some of the people return to the promised land and live there as "Yehud"—a province of the Persian Empire.

Where in the Bible: Jeremiah, Ezekiel, Isaiah 40–55, Lamentations, Psalm 137, Daniel, Esther.

This sounds much more interesting than the random verses that have made it into a sermon.

THE ACOLYTE

The Province "Yehud" in the Persian Empire— Time Period: 539–333 BCE

When Cyrus of Persia says the people can return home, many (but not all) do so, and they begin to rebuild their lives. Under the high priest Yeshua, the people return, rebuild the temple, and restore worship. Under the priest Ezra, the book of the law of Moses is read aloud to the people. Under Nehemiah, a governor appointed by the Persians, the walls of Jerusalem are rebuilt. Great hardships ensue—the return is not as rosy as the people had expected. Famine, conflict, religious dispute, and other hardships plague the people. Prophets appear, as in the past, to preach both hope and obedience—the anonymous prophet known as Third Isaiah, Haggai, Zechariah, and Malachi. The people become a people of law (in the best sense of that word) and religious devotion, ruled by priests and governors—rather than a nation ruled by a king. In some ways, this is a return to what God originally intended—a people ruled directly by the Lord.

Where in the Bible: Ezra, Nehemiah, Isaiah 56–66, Haggai, Zechariah, Malachi.

The Province of Judea in Hellenistic and Roman Times—Time Period: 333–4 BCE

The Protestant Old Testament story ends with the restoration of the walls of Jerusalem, although portions of the Old Testament were written many years later. The book of Daniel, for instance, though it recounts stories from the time of the exile and just after, was actually written about 167 BCE. During the centuries between the restoration of Jerusalem and the birth of Jesus around the year 4 BCE, what we call Second-Temple Judaism (to be distinguished from later Rabbinic Judaism) continues to disperse across the ancient world. Those people who remain in the promised land continue to develop and preserve their Scriptures and religion. At times, the people are left to live in peace within the empires under which they live. At other times, the people are oppressed. Empires come and go— the Persians are replaced by the Greeks, who give way to the Seleucids and the Ptolemies, and then finally to the legions of Rome. But as the ages turn, the people of God remain.

Where in the Bible: These events and stories are not in the Protestant Old Testament/Jewish Bible. But many relevant stories can be read in the apocryphal writings, especially 1–4 Maccabees.

Other Writings in the Old Testament

So, dear reader, if you have been reading carefully, you may have noticed that a handful of Old Testament books are not listed in the preceding history of the Old Testament. The reason is simple: some Old Testament books do not fit into the history because they are timeless. They were not written to fit into any one period of Israel's history. Some of them are lyrical poetry, for which no precise time or location is necessary for them to make sense. Some are books of wisdom meditating on the proper order—or lack thereof—in creation or society.

The Book of Psalms

The most important of the remaining books is Psalms. Although some psalms were listed above because they have clear references either to creation or to Israel's history, most of the psalms are poems of faith. Some express the pain of life in hauntingly delicate prayers or excruciatingly articulate laments. Some sing praise of Israel's deliverer with joy that is both spontaneous and infectious. Some express the most confident trust, even in the midst of life's most paralyzing dangers. Some leap off the page with words of thanksgiving and gratitude in response to experiences of salvation that echo across the millennia. And some teach about the life of faith with the wisdom of a well-traveled elder.

The Books of Proverbs and Ecclesiastes

These two reflective books are the good-cop, bad-cop wisdom books from Israel's library. The good-cop book— Proverbs—sees the glass of wisdom as half full. The creation is trustworthy, well-ordered, and you can figure it out. Sometimes it sounds like a favorite coach or music teacher, sometimes like your mom or grandma. Sometimes it is funny, other times a little boring. The bad-cop book—Ecclesiastes—looks over Proverbs's shoulder and scoffs at its naïveté and mocks its innocence. "The race isn't always to the swift," its author scolds. And a great deal of life is vanity. Sometimes the best one can do is enjoy a good meal and having one's deepest prejudices confirmed.

The Song of Songs

Like a good rom-com? Or a cheesy romance novel? How about a sexually suggestive dramatic script? Well, then the Song of Songs is for you. Originally, it might have been just an erotic drama about young love between two passionate lovers—a young male and young female—betrothed to each other. Its inclusion in the Bible was controversial—the relationship between God and God's people is often compared in the Old Testament to the love of a husband and a wife. Sometimes that relationship is only described as a troubled relationship beset by betrayal, distrust, sin, and punishment. If this love story is read against that background, it's nice to know that the relationship between God and the people can be one of pure joy—of pure desire: God's desire for us and our desire for God.

THE DEACON

Read this with teenagers if you don't pick up on all the suggestive imagery.

The Book of Job

Last, but certainly not least in importance, is the book of Job. This story tells the tale of a mythical man from the east named Job who is both the most righteous person *ever* and also the most unfortunate sufferer *ever*. The book wonders, "How can this be? How can a person be both righteous and suffer?" Because we all know that only the unrighteous suffer, right? People only get what they deserve, right? Well, obviously not. But a lot of people throughout the ages have thought that. This book takes a long, hard look at that question and also at religious responses to suffering. But more on that later—after you've suffered through a couple hundred pages of this book.

2

A Down-and-Dirty Creator—A Downright-Broken Creation

Sometimes, when you're tackling a difficult question or a really big topic, the best place to start is the beginning. When tackling the Old Testament and wrestling with the really big question of God, the beginning is definitely a good place to start. As in, The Beginning. The beginning of creation, the beginning of life, the beginning of the universe.

Summary of Genesis 1–11

Let's consider the first eleven chapters of Genesis as The Beginning. Here's a quick overview.

The First Creation Story (Genesis 1)—Creation by Speech in Seven Days

In the first creation story in the Old Testament, God speaks creation into existence in six days and rests on the seventh. Notice how there is a connection between days 1 and 4, 2 and 5, and 3 and 6.

Day 1—God speaks in the darkness and creates light.

Day 4—God speaks and creates the stars, sun, and moon to populate the heavens.

Day 2—God speaks and creates the earthly environment, with air and water.

Day 5—God speaks and creates living creatures to populate the sea and the air.

Day 3—God speaks and creates the dry land in the midst of the air and water; God speaks again to create plants.

Day 6—God speaks and creates living creatures to populate the earth; God speaks again to create humankind in God's image—every male and female human is in God's image.

Day 7—God rests.

The Second Creation Story (Genesis 2)—Creation in the Garden

In the second creation story, the Lord God forms the human being from the dust of the earth and breathes life in the human. Then the Lord God places the human being in the garden with the purpose to "till and keep it" but with the commandment not to eat from the tree of the knowledge of good and evil. Then, noting that "it is not good that the human should be alone," the Lord God creates every animal and brings them one by one to the human being to name and to see if there is a fitting life partner for him. But none of the animals are fitting, so the Lord God creates "the mother of life" from the very body of the human being—and thus male and female are created—Adam and Eve.

I asked my fundamentalist brother-in-law how his creationism makes sense of both creation stories in Genesis. Some questions are best left unasked.

THE ELDER

The Rebellion (Genesis 3)—Human Beings Want to "Be Like God"

The third story in the Bible is often called "the fall from grace," because the human beings violate the Lord God's commandment. The snake—the craftiest of God's creatures—promises the woman that if they eat from the tree of the knowledge of good and evil, "you will be like God, knowing good and evil." The woman and man do eat from the tree, and indeed, they now know good and evil. They experience shame, they fashion crude clothing for themselves to cover their nakedness, and they hide from God. The Lord God realizes what has happened and punishes them by casting them out of the garden. As a consequence of sin, the man must struggle with the earth to wrestle the means for survival from the soil. The woman must struggle in childbirth to give birth to the next generation so that the species may survive. And the snake and human beings will be in constant enmity with each other.

Life, Death, and Sin (Genesis 4a)—The First Family and First Murder

Adam and Eve settle down and have a couple of kids. Cain, the first born, likes plants. Abel, the second born, likes animals. They both offer the Lord sacrifices, but the Lord likes the animal sacrifice better than the plant—we don't know why. Remember that part about knowing good from evil? Well, knowing good from evil doesn't mean that humans have the ability to choose good instead of evil. So what does Cain do? He kills Abel in fit of jealousy. As a result, God banishes Cain. Cain goes away, marries, and starts his own family. Adam and Eve have another son, and the human race grows.

Begetting and Begetting, Part I (Genesis 4b–5)— Lots of Kids

In the second part of Genesis 4 and through Genesis 5, lots of people have lots of sex and have lots of kids. People live long lives and then die. More sex, more people. Not much else happens.

> Trivia, part 1: Jubal was the father of music—I'm pretty sure he preferred classic rock (it was the stone age, after all).

> Trivia, part 2: The oldest person on the list is named Methuselah—969 years.

I am glad to hear Jubal liked rock. Barth had me scared of heaven with all his Mozart and Bach talk.

THE ELDER

The technical name for these lists of people having sex and offspring is *genealogy*. The technical euphemism for having sex is "to know." Thus, "the man knew his wife Eve" (Genesis 4:1) means that they had sex. Thus the phrase "to know in the biblical sense," which means having sex. Who knew!? Well, in this passage, Adam and Eve knew . . . in the biblical sense.

But how much knowing is too much knowing before marriage?

THE ACOLYTE

The Big Flood (Genesis 6–9)—A Not-So-Gentle Kid's Story

Then "the Lord saw that the wickedness of humankind was great in the earth, and that every inclination of the thoughts of their hearts was only evil continually" (Genesis 6:5). And so, God sends a flood to destroy creation.

But God notices Noah and realizes that there's some good in creation. So God downloads for Noah some plans for a giant floating box in which to preserve two of every kind of animal. And Noah and his family weather the great flood in the big box. As soon as the flood is over, Noah gets hammered drunk and passes out naked. Oh well. Sin still exits.

Begetting and Begetting, Part II (Genesis 10)— Lots More Kids

In Genesis 10, lots of people have lots of sex and have lots more kids. People live shorter and shorter lives.

> Trivia, part 3: Nimrod is the first mighty warrior and hunter.

THE DEACON

Nimrod is also the album title for what punk rock band?

The Big Tower (Genesis 11a)—God Confuses the Languages

In the first part of Genesis 11, the humans still want to be like God. They try to build a mighty city and a tower to heaven. God scatters the people and confuses their languages.

Begetting and Begetting, Part III (Genesis 11b)— Lots and Lots More Kids

In the second part of Genesis 11, you guessed it, more sex and more kids. No trivia. Apparently the confusion of the language ended the trivia for a while.

God Is Law—God Brings about a Trustworthy Creation

By now you may be wondering: What kind of literature is this? I mean, God speaking reality into existence, then digging around in a garden, breathing life into a dirt man, snakes talking, brother murdering brother? What's up? Well, let's come back to that really perceptive question in a little bit. But first, how about a look at some of the more important themes of the first eleven chapters of the Old Testament.

CHAPTER 2, OPTIONAL QUEST #1: READ GENESIS 1 (COMPLETE QUEST AND LEVEL UP TO OT RECRUIT, FIRST CLASS).

The first crucially important theme is that *God is a God of law*. And, furthermore, the purpose of God's law is life—the very existence of creation and the existence within creation of life.

Take a closer look at a few of the words for God's actions in Genesis 1. According to the verbs, God does a few things in the first chapter of the Old Testament.

THE DEACON

Role-Playing Game references make me happy. Should I go grab my D20? (That's a twenty-sided dice for all ye Dungeons & Dragons newbies.)

Remember that most of the Old Testament is written in ancient Hebrew, so there are a few references to the Hebrew verbs. In order of occurrence:

- God "separated" and "divided" and "gathered together"
- God made heavenly lights to "rule" over the day and night
- God "blessed" humanity to "subdue and have dominion" over the living creation

All of these verbs describe the ways in which the Creator works through law, through ordering, and through the gathering of energy . . . all for the purpose of bringing a *trustworthy and life-giving* creation. This is a theme that we will return to throughout this book. But it is a critical theme already in the very first chapter of the Old Testament. *The Creator is a God of law. Through the law—here it is the natural law—God works to bring about a trustworthy creation that can sustain and nurture life.*

Reflect on this point for a moment. In order for the creation to exist—and even more importantly, for there to be a life-supporting environment within the vastness of creation—natural law must exist. God's very first act of creation is to bring order—through natural law—into the universe in order that a trustworthy and life-supporting creation might exist. God sustains creation from moment to moment. From instant to instant, God's very being holds creation together, sustaining natural law and nurturing life. One might even say that God is not a thing—not a noun—God is a verb. God sustains, God effects natural law; one might almost say that God is law itself.

If God is a verb, can I do God? That might be less awkward than knowing God . . . biblically.

THE ACOLYTE

The Creative Process—Peaceful, Nonviolent . . . Loving

In the Old Testament, the Creator God is one God. *The* Creator. It isn't done by a committee. And God the Creator is not a tortured, confused artist, searching for motivation and unsure how best to proceed.

Well, maybe God *is* a tortured genius artist. What I meant to write was: God the Creator is not a torturer—not violent. No being has to die in order to bring about creation. The creative act is peaceful. At least in the sense that neither God nor some other being dies in order to

create life. And human beings are God's beloved creatures—created in God's image.

And here's the shocking news: the Creator is peaceful
and loving. Creation is a peaceful act. And human beings
are created in God's image, blessed to continue God's work.

To get a sense of how shocking this news might have
once sounded to ancient ears, it might be helpful to hear a
little bit about what Israel's neighbors thought about creation. Among Israel's neighbors, the act of creation was
almost universally imagined as an act of violence, in which
one god slew at least one other god or goddess.

In the Enuma Elish, which is the creation story of
Israel's neighbors in the Mesopotamian valley, creation is
committee work. Probably a church committee. Which
explains why creation is also a violent process, certain
members of the committee resorting to conflict. The creation epic describes how the two originating gods, Apsu
and Tiamat (representing fresh water and salt water), give
life to other gods—thus forming the committee. A conflict then arises in the creation committee, which results
in the death of both Apsu and Tiamat. The hero Marduk
slays Tiamat: "He seized the spear and burst her belly /
He severed her inward parts, he pierced (her) heart."
Then, "From her body, Marduk created heaven and later
humanity, to be the servants of the gods."

Creation myths among Israel's other neighbors were
similar. Creation was a committee job, usually requiring
the death of one or more committee members. If I had been
forced to serve on a committee with Marduk and Tiamat, I
would have volunteered for death. So boring, those two. It
is also worth noting that the role human beings play in the

I am always thrilled to know a dead mother's body wasn't necessary for God to create.

THE BISHOP

creation stories of Israel's neighbors was often described as the servants or slaves of the gods.

Notice how different Israel's God is. There is no violence. God simply speaks, and creation is spoken into existence. Creation is an act of linguistic order. And note that the verbs *create* and *made* and *bring forth* and *blessed* are positive and peaceful words of creation, of world construction, and, we can even say, of love. The human beings are in God's image; human beings are not God's slaves.

Let's review. (1) Creation is by one God, not a committee. (2) Creation is peaceful—nobody has to get tortured or die. (3) Human beings are in God's image, not imagined as God's slaves. (4) Your little cousins are irritating.

Creation—A One-and-Done Miracle, but a Now-and-Ongoing Process

On the one hand, Genesis 1 presents creation as the one-and-done miracle, solely commissioned and effected by the one God. On the other hand, it presents creation as the ongoing process through which God uses what has already been created in order to keep on keeping on with the creating thing.

The verb *created*—*bara'* in Hebrew—is the very first word of the Bible in Hebrew. And throughout the Old Testament, only God is the subject of this verb. Only God creates. Only God *can* create. The act of forming something out of nothing, of ordering the random chaos of the sea into the land and air and life, of shaping the quarks, neutrinos, and atoms into molecules and cells and elephants—only God can do that. And the original act of creation happened once.

On the other hand, notice these phrases:

- "Let the earth put forth vegetation, plants yielding seeds and trees of every kind bearing fruit with the seed in it." (Genesis 1:11)
- "Let the waters bring forth swarms of living creatures, and let birds fly above the earth. . . . Be fruitful and multiply and fill the waters in the seas, and let birds multiply on the earth." (Genesis 1:20–22)
- "Let the earth bring forth living creatures of every kind." (Genesis 1:24)
- [To humanity] "Be fruitful and multiply and fill the earth and subdue it." (Genesis 1:28)

God uses some of the things that God created to continue the creative process. God created the earth, which brings forth vegetation—which has in it seeds, through which the next generation of vegetation will be created. God created the water, which brings forth the living creatures of the seas. These marine animals and the birds of the air are "fruitful and multiply," creating the next generation to fill the seas and the air. God again uses the earth to bring forth living creatures of every sort, including humanity. All of these creatures once again are "fruitful and multiply," continuing the creation's life.

At this point, I imagine plenty of God's other creatures are hoping we dial back the multiply part.

THE ELDER

The crown of God's creation, according to Genesis 1, is humanity. Only humanity is created "in God's image." What this means is not precisely clear. Since God is not visible, it does not mean that human beings look like God. Rather, it means that humanity shares some key characteristic or characteristics with God. One possibility for this characteristic is *creativity*. In Genesis 1, God creates. Human beings thus are God's "created cocreators." We have an ability to create that goes beyond other animals. Another possibility is that humans share the capacity for language with God. In Genesis 1, God speaks. Human beings, alone among God's creatures, have the capacity for advanced language (and writing). A third possibility is that human beings share with God a spiritual heart. It says elsewhere in Scripture that "God is Spirit." Human beings, perhaps alone among God's creations, are spiritual—we have a "God-shaped hole" in our souls, some people argue, which only God can fill (if your God is love, that would make the hole heart-shaped; if your God is a donut . . .). If we fill it with other things—false gods such as fame, money, power, pleasure, alcohol or drugs, food, beauty, even self-sacrifice—we will never truly be satisfied. Still another possibility is the ability to form complex civilizations and to govern the rest of the earthly creation. The text says, "God created humankind in his image . . . [and said], 'fill the earth and subdue it; and have dominion over'" the rest of creation. Human beings share the divine capacity to form civilization and govern. Perhaps it is all of these things. Perhaps it's something else. The answer is elusive.

The Down-and-Dirty Creator

In the second creation story in Genesis, the Lord God gets down and dirty, breathing life and planting purpose into humanity. The two creation stories are only two of many passages in the Old Testament that describe creation. Others include Job 38–41 and Psalms 8, 104, and 139—and there are more. These different stories are meant to complement each other—they are not in competition.

> CHAPTER 2, OPTIONAL QUEST #2: READ GENESIS 2–4 (COMPLETE QUEST AND LEVEL UP TO OT RECRUIT, SECOND CLASS).

Several enlightening wordplays—puns and charged words—call for our attention in Genesis 2. Working with those wordplays is perhaps the most promising way to get at the significant message of the chapter.

The Earthling from the Earth

In the most well-known pun in the Bible, God forms the earthling from the earth: "The Lord God formed the human from the dust of the ground, and breathed into his nostrils the breath of life; and the man became a living being" (Genesis 2:7). The Hebrew plays on the words for *man* or *human*—*adam*—and *ground* or *earth*—*adamah*. The *adam* is formed from the *adamah*. There are clever ways to try to give a sense of the meaning in English. The earthling is formed from the earth (Spock would like that one). The human is formed from the *humus* (but isn't that a dip that goes with pita bread?). My personal favorite is that God forms the dirtbag from the dirt (which seems to describe most people pretty accurately).

These wordplays score several important points here. First, a scientific-reality point—our bodies come from the earth and are made up of earthly stuff (we are mostly made up of oxygen, hydrogen, and carbon). This point is expanded when God "breathed the breath of life into his nostrils" (the first recorded act of CPR). You are what you eat, drink, and also what you breathe. Second, an environmental point—we are made up of the earth, so we better take care of it. As goes our ecosystem, so goes humanity. This point is extended a couple of verses later when we are reminded that "out of the ground the Lord God made to grow every tree that is pleasant to the sight and good for food" (Genesis 2:9). Third, a theological point—we come from the dust and will return to the dust. On Ash Wednesday every year, Christians hear the words, "Remember you are dust and to dust you shall return." You might want to consider eternity right now—you are going to die someday—and get right with your Creator.

THE ACOLYTE

Ash Wednesday is my favorite service of the year because it is the only time I am sure we are telling the truth. We are going to die.

To Till and to Keep

Genesis 2 also includes several highly charged theological words. One important pair of those words comes in the description of the human being's purpose in the garden: "The Lord God took the man and put him in the garden of Eden to till it and keep it" (2:15). These words indicate that humanity is the servant of creation. In Genesis 1, the metaphors for the role of humanity with creation are metaphors of lordship and power over—we are "to subdue the earth" and "exercise dominion" over the works of God's hand. In Genesis 2, the metaphors are of servanthood and power under—we are to serve creation and safeguard it.

On the more individual level of meaning, it is worth noting that every human being needs purpose. And we find that purpose in serving others. Jesus said that "human beings do not live by bread alone" (Matthew 4:4). When I was in college, one of my friends had a poster in his dorm room of a beer mug and the older translation of that verse underneath it: "Man does not live by bread alone." In addition to the basics of life—food, shelter, clothing, your smart phone—we also need higher spiritual things. Jesus says we need the "word of God." Oh, goooooooood for you, Jesus. But we could add a few other metaphysical things. In addition to the basics, we need friendship, community, love. And Genesis 2:15 would add, we need purpose. We find that purpose most powerfully when we learn to serve others and to love them.

By the way, this chapter also says that we need beauty. Note that "the Lord God made to grow every tree that is pleasant to the sight and good for food." We need food, purpose, but also beauty. God made creation to include things that are "pleasant to the sight." Or, for my taste also, "pleasant to the ear." My idea of beauty? A great day at the lake, my wife by my side, and a good John Prine song. And, of course, all John Prine songs are good.

A Life Partner

I just mentioned my wife. My life partner. My honey. In addition to the basics of life, in addition to purpose, in addition to beauty, human beings are meant to be in relationship with each other.

Genesis 2 includes this rather comic scene: Doing his job of serving and safeguarding, the poor man is lonely. And the Lord God declares, "It is not good that the man should be alone. I will make for him a helper-partner as his complement." The word *ezer*—traditionally translated as helpmate, helpmeet, or simply helper—*does not imply a lesser or hierarchically subservient role*, as these traditional renderings sort of imply. The being most often called *ezer* in the Old Testament is none other than the Lord God—hardly a subservient figure!

THE BISHOP

Since the fellas spent a couple thousand years insisting *ezer* justified patriarchy, I am happy to compromise for just a thousand years of women's status being just below the hardly subservient Lord God.

Genesis 1 and 2 complement each other. In Genesis 1, seven times God sees that the creation is good seven times. And each time, it's always the complementary relational completeness of the creation that is good. Darkness and light are good; sky and water and earth are good; plants where you eat the outside and plants where you eat the inside are good; the sun to rule the day and the moon and stars to rule the night are good; and so on. Always in complement. But in Genesis 2, where the man has no helper-partner as a complement, the Lord God announces, it is not good.

Human beings need other human beings. We were made to be in community with each other and with God. The most basic form of human community is the family—traditionally, multiple generations living together. But community includes not only family. It is friendship. Comradeship. Work partners. Neighbors. Nerd pals who play Settlers of Catan together on the porch of the cabin. We all need community! That's how God made us.

What is Settlers of
Catan?

THE ELDER

Come on over, Elder;
I've been looking
forward to playing
Settlers of Catan all
WHEAT!

THE DEACON

Furthermore, notice that in Genesis 1 it's God who does the naming. God calls the light *day* and the darkness *night*. God calls the dome *sky* and the dry earth *land*. In Genesis 2, God forms new creatures and brings them to the man to see what the man will call them, what the man will name them. One insight from this story is that naming things is a capacity we share with God. We are the only creatures who share the Creator's capacity to use language. And language allows knowledge to advance, to be stored up for the next generation; it allows us to be scientific. This is part of our human vocation—to name, to know, to learn, to grow, to invent and create. And that naming and knowing and inventing is part of our common human calling.

Now with all of that context in place, let the rather comic scene begin. And fortunately, through the magic of digital technology, I have been able to reconstruct the scene as it actually happened.

The Lord God digs into the dirt and forms an animal with four long legs, an elongated snout, and a hairy mane and brings it to the man, where it says, "Neighhhhhhhh!" And the man says, "You are not fit to be a helper-partner as my complement. I shall call you *Horse*!"

The Lord God digs into the dirt and forms an animal with four medium-length legs; it chews the cud, has cloven hooves, and makes pleasant milk. The Lord God brings it to the man, where it says, "Mooooooooo!" And the man says, "You are not fit to be a helper-partner as my complement. I shall call you *Cow*!"

The Lord God digs into the dirt and forms an animal that doesn't sweat and that has four short legs, a snubby snout, and a curly tail. The Lord God brings it to the man, where it says, "Oink!" And the man says, "You are not fit to be a helper-partner as my complement. I shall call you *Breakfast*!" (Wow—that is a really funny but really culturally insensitive joke. This story does come from ancient Israel, whose people did not eat pigs. Sorry. But really. All the best breakfasts include bacon—the candy of the meat family.)

And so it goes, over and over, and among all the animals, from the field mouse all the way up to the elephant, there is found no help-partner to be the man's complement.

And so we see the Lord God weave a second layer of the relational web. Like God, we name, we use language, we categorize, and we are capable of critical thinking; we preserve our wisdom for future generations. We are part of the same creation as the animals, but we are different. The animals can provide companionship, and we exist symbiotically with them. But they are not us.

Then, of course, the Lord God finally forms woman. And when the man sees her, he says, "Now that's what I'm talking about!!"

Amen! I've tried being a vegetarian three times, and it was always bacon that lured me back. Of

THE ELDER

course, there were no factory-farming documentaries on Netflix in the days of Adam.

Actually he says, "this at last is bone of my bone, flesh of my flesh." And I don't think I need my friends from the Hebrew Dictionary store to tell me what that means. It was a cultural idiom—that is, a weird phrase that everyone understood. To say that something is "bone of my bone" meant something was perfectly suited for you. The joke is that in the story, God makes the woman from one of the man's "bones." So she is literally "bone of my bone." Is there a sexual element to the joke? Probably.

More than one.

THE ACOLYTE

But let's not miss the point. The lonely man, who needs community, looks at the woman and says, "Now that's what I'm talking about!!"

And then the scene ends with the summary judgment: "Therefore a man leaves his father and mother and cleaves to his wife and they become one flesh." Again, a sexual joke? Sure. But also a point about family, about community, about the need for relationship.

Genesis 2 gives us a picture of a complex, relational web of creation in which human beings live and in which they find meaning, purpose, and identity. The most intimate of relational rings are our human-to-human relationships with one another. And most intimately, the relational uniting of male and female through which the Lord God works again and again to create the next generation and, as Psalm 104 says, sends for the divine Spirit to renew the face of the earth.

God has fashioned us to be in relationship with the earth, the animal kingdom, with other human beings, and even with God. In that incredibly complex yet transparently visible web, God has called you and me to live lives that matter. So think about this creation story also as a call story. God is saying to you: "I am calling you to live a life that is free, and that is loving, and that has purpose, and in which you have vital relationships with other people, with animals and plants, and most of all, with me—your down-and-dirty Creator."

Now that's what I'm talking about!

The Original Sin—The Plot of the Entire Bible

So after two chapters of the Bible, we have a picture of a perfectly balanced creation. Goodness is described as complementary balance—when everything in creation has its place, everything in creation is in place, and everything in creation is doing what it is supposed to do.

New England Patriots football coach Bill Belichick is famous for the mantra, "Do your job." That is how creation was supposed to work. Everyone staying in their own lane, doing their job.

I feel a bit deflated after a Belichick reference.

THE ELDER

The Elder assumes everyone reading this is aware that Belichick is the head coach of one

THE BISHOP

of the most successful cheating teams in NFL history. Not everyone knows how they were busted filming other teams' practices or deflating footballs so they were easier to throw.

In the Bible, that lasted for two chapters. Then, in the third chapter, a couple of people decided that they wanted to do someone else's job. Here's how it went:

The snake was more devious than any other wild animal that the Lord God had made. He said to the woman, "Did God really say, 'You shall not eat from any tree in the garden?'" The woman said to the snake, "We may eat from any tree in the garden, but from the fruit of the tree in the middle of the garden, God said, 'You must not eat from it, you must not touch it, lest you die.'" But the snake said to the woman, "You won't die. God knows that on the day when you eat from it, your eyes will open up. You will be like God— knowing good from evil!" (Genesis 3:1–5)

And you know the rest. If you leave two five-year-olds in a room with one hundred toys and say to them, "I have to go fix a snack. While I'm gone, you can play with these ninety-nine toys on the floor, but that one toy on the shelf—don't play with that one; it's special. I'll be right back." As soon you close the door, both of those urchins will go straight for the toy on the shelf. So maybe it was God's fault—if God hadn't told them not to eat of the fruit of the tree of the knowledge of good and evil, they never would have even wanted to.

But this story really isn't about whether or not you should tempt humans by giving them a rule. After all, this is a story with a talking snake and a tree with magical fruit that if you eat, you'll suddenly know stuff you didn't know before. Maybe God should have made a tree that gave people the knowledge of which sports are good and which are evil. "For in the day that you eat of it, you shall know that the Green Bay Packers, Manchester United, and the New York Yankees sucketh."

This story is a parable about what is wrong with the world. And what is wrong with the world? First, people don't stay in their lane! The snake takes on God's role of

What about God's preferential option for the Purple and Gold? #Lakers #Vikings

THE DEACON

giving commandments and making promises. And the woman—and her husband—decide that they "wanted to be like God, knowing good from evil."

Oddly enough, when Cain and Abel asked Adam why they were no longer in the garden of Eden, he said, "Your mother ate us out of house and home."

THE DEACON

How many cheesy Bible jokes do you have?

THE ACOLYTE

Sometimes the act of eating the fruit is called the *original sin*. That is, it was the first sin. The point of the story is that something is deeply wrong with God's creation.

Before *sins* were things that we do or fail to do, *sin* was a condition into which we were all born. Sin is the situation in which we find ourselves—that creation is broken. We are all born into a world where things are not as we imagine they should be if there is a good and gracious God. People die. People kill and oppress each other. Our bodies fail us—cancer and many other awful illnesses strike innocent people down. This story is a parable describing the world as a broken place.

This story is also sometimes called . . . dun, Dun, DUN! . . . *The Fall*. As in, human beings were made to live in a state of grace in close relationship with God, but they sinned and they *fell* from grace. The fall is a long-accepted way to understand this story.

But a competing way to understand this story is to think of it not as a fall downward but as a *rebellion upward*. The man and woman are not content to live in the roles that God intended for them. They *want to be like God*. Rather than staying in their lane, they decide to eat of the magical fruit that gives them the ability to know right from wrong. And so they do. And they know right from wrong.

But, sadly, the ability to know right from wrong does not give a person the ability to *choose* right instead of wrong. Nor does the ability to know right from wrong necessarily give a person the wisdom to achieve what is right rather than wrong—even when you try to achieve what is right.

An example. In Genesis 4, Cain Adamson kills his brother Abel Adamson. Why? Because God preferred Abel's sacrifice to Cain's sacrifice. Abel's sacrifice was an animal sacrifice—it came from the flock. Cain's sacrifice

Yet knowing right from wrong is not without its perks. It does enable me to spot just how deplorable other people are, and that (regretfully of course) is enjoyable.

THE ELDER

was a plant—it came from the ground. Why did God prefer one over the other? The text doesn't say. Maybe God prefers meat to vegetables. I do. Maybe Cain's sacrifice came from the ground, which had been cursed by God as a result of human sin. Or maybe it was just that on that particular day God on a whim just liked one sacrifice better.

Are you sure God wasn't on the Paleo Diet?

THE BISHOP

So what does Cain do? Out of jealousy, Cain kills Abel. Does he know it's wrong? Yep. His parents had eaten of the tree of the knowledge of good and evil. He knows murdering another human is always wrong, even when it's your annoying brother. And he does it anyway.

The ability to know good from evil does not mean that we have the ability to *choose* good over evil. If it did, Cain would not have killed Abel. And I would not prefer the taste of bacon to the taste of kale. I mean, I know that kale is better for me than bacon, but it doesn't have that salty, crispy crunch of fat!

THE ACOLYTE

I'm vegan and the meat talk is making my tummy turn. Weren't Adam and Eve pre-fall vegetarians?

According to the story, from the day the two humans ate of the fruit of the tree, they became mortal. One way to understand the meaning of the phrase, "God said, 'You must not eat from it, you must not touch it, lest you die,'" is that "lest you die" means "lest you become mortal." Which we are. So if you've ever felt robbed by a loved one's death of feared your own death, you have felt the result of eating the fruit.

And notice the power of shame. Perhaps no social power is more powerful than the negative power of shame and the positive power of honor. Before eating of the fruit, "the man and his wife were naked, and were not ashamed" (Genesis 2:25). After becoming aware of good and evil, however, "they became aware that they were naked, so they sewed together fig-tree leaves and made underwear for themselves . . . and they hid from the presence of the Lord God" (Genesis 3:7–8).

If you have ever experienced shame—being mocked, ridiculed, pilloried, publicly excluded, or humiliated in front of others—you know its power. "You can't eat with us." "Take that, you loser!" "You're fired! This security officer will escort you out the front door; do the walk of shame." If you've ever experienced that, you know the power of shame. You have felt the result of eating the fruit.

After God discovers that they have eaten the fruit, the first thing that the man does is throw his wife under the bus. God: "Who told you that you are naked? Did you eat of the fruit of the tree I told you not to?" The man: "The woman! The one you gave to me! She gave the fruit to me and I ate it." So another result of knowing good from evil is the ability to make up a good excuse, even if it throws your loved one under the bus. Ever been blamed for something? Ever been betrayed? Ever been left alone to hold the bag for a group's crime? You have felt the result of eating the fruit.

The number of "blame the wife" jokes inspired by this story frustrates me.

THE BISHOP

Earlier, I mentioned that this story describes the broken condition—the condition of sin—into which each

THE ELDER

Well Bishop, with enough graduate school you can outsource all your own agency to some system, parent, -ism, video game, demon, or current blood-sugar level.

of us is born. One way that this story portrays our broken condition is by describing the consequences of eating the fruit. In addition to knowing right from wrong, God imposes other consequences for breaking God's commandment.

The story describes these consequences as *curses*.

First, God curses the snake: "You are cursed among animals. . . . I will put enmity between you and the woman, and between your offspring and hers" (Genesis 3:14–15). Traditionally, the snake has been understood as the devil—the being whose lies led the woman and man to rebel against God. Second, God curses the woman: "I will greatly increase your pangs in childbirth. . . . Your husband shall rule over you" (3:16). Here, the story is saying that the fact that childbirth is painful, that women must sweat and endure pain in order to pass life to the next generation—this, too, is a part of the brokenness of creation. Third, God curses the man: "Cursed is the ground because of you, only through toil shall you eat of it all the days of your life. . . . Only through the sweat of your face shall you eat food until you return to the ground" (3:17–19). Here, the story is saying that the fact that the human race must work hard to wrestle the means of survival from the ground—this, too, is part of the brokenness of creation. Procuring the means to survive should not be this hard in a good creation. Fourth, the mortality of all life is likewise part of the brokenness of creation: "you are dust and to dust you shall return" (3:19). And fifth, human separation from God is part of the brokenness of creation. The people were banished from the garden, sent out from the presence of God.

But there is an ameliorating blessing from God as they leave. God gives them proper clothing—God "clothed them." Since there isn't a Macy's around where they can go and pop some tags—and since they don't have either the tools or skills to make their own clothes—the gift of proper clothing is no small blessing.

Oh, and a final pun. Adam named his wife Eve—*chivah* in Hebrew—because she was the mother of all life—*chay* in Hebrew. From *chivah* came *chay*.

And there you have the plot of the entire Bible: sin and a good and loving Creator. God created a world out of love, to be in balance and harmony, with everyone staying in their lane and doing their job. But creation went wrong. It's broken. So the question is—What is a good

THE BISHOP

That is the question. The challenge is how you lead a congregation to ask it and feel its weight in a secular age.

and gracious God, committed to love and justice, going to do with a creation that is broken? Good question.

A Quick Word about Cain and Abel and Seth and Their Wives and Cities

Let's return very briefly to the story of Cain and Abel. After Cain kills Abel, God judges Cain for his monstrous crime. Just as Adam and Even had been banished from the garden, so Cain is banished.

> Cain protested, "My sin is greater than I can bear! . . . I shall be a fugitive and a wanderer on the earth, and anyone who meets me may kill me." Then the Lord said to him, "Not so! Anyone who kills Cain will suffer a sevenfold vengeance." And the Lord put a mark on Cain, so that no one who came upon him would kill him. (Genesis 4:13–15)

The "mark of Cain" is a blessing—a promise of protection. It is a blessing that keeps him—who has slain his own brother—from being killed. So then Cain goes away, has a son, and builds a city.

THE ACOLYTE

Isn't it a bit weird God is against capital punishment for Cain but cool drowning all but one family of humans?

Notice again this pattern: Sin (murder) → Consequence (banishment) → Blessing (the mark).

As was the case with Adam and Eve, the pattern of sin, consequence, and blessing occurs. It is worth noting that we are not told what the "mark of Cain" was. Was it a tattoo? The first ink? Was it a birthmark? The ancient Jewish rabbis had fun imaging what the sign might been. One rabbi said he was given a dog, another said a horn grew from his head, another said it was a Hebrew letter. We are not told—just that it was to keep Cain from being murdered.

It is also important to note that the phrase "the mark of Cain" has a vile history of being used in racist, anti-Semitic, and oppressive ways. In America, some early Christians picked up on a long history of interpretation that dated far back in the Christian tradition and said it was dark skin color. This misidentification then led some Southern Christians to use the "curse of Cain" as justification for enslaving African Americans. Thus, they turned the blessing Cain was given into a curse. In Europe, the "mark of Cain" was sometimes used against Jews. There is much to repent for.

A final question—where did all these people who are going to murder Cain come from? If there are only four people—Adam, Eve, Cain, Abel—and Cain had killed Abel, who is Cain afraid of? And where does Cain's wife come from? And how does Cain build a city—who would live there? The only thing I can say for the moment is this—the people who preserved this story were not all at bothered by those questions. They simply didn't care about such matters.

But again, one wonders, what kind of literature is this?

Should God Have Started Over?

Now we turn to one of the most beloved, most picturesque, most brutal, most terrifying, and yet most promising stories in Genesis. The story of the great flood.

It's funny how artists of children's books and makers of children's toys love this story. When my daughter was born, we were given a mobile of the flood story to hang over her crib, a plastic toy of the ark and animals to play with, a children's Bible that included this story, even a sewn-cloth toy book to bring to church to keep her busy while we pray.

Here's the message: "Play around with this story about God deciding to kill every living being in creation—it's cute."

I need to confess something. For many years, as an Old Testament scholar, I had no idea what to make of this terrifying story. I had no idea if there was any good news at all in this story. But in the end, I think I finally understood what the story is about and where the good news is.

The good news of this story is to be found in what it tells us about God's character and God's way of dealing with sin—of dealing with a creation that is broken.

Because the story tells us that God is a God of both justice and mercy, God's sense of justice is acute. And God's commitment to mercy is even more acute. And both of these—justice and mercy—are aspects of God's love.

In my biblical-literalist days, I actually brought a bunch of extra felt-board animals into Sunday

THE DEACON

school just to drown them. You never want to miss a chance to warn six-year-olds about how much wrath God has for sinners . . . oh, and next time it's with fire!!

CHAPTER 2, OPTIONAL QUEST #3: READ GENESIS 6:5–9:27 (COMPLETE QUEST AND LEVEL UP TO OT RECRUIT, THIRD CLASS).

The story gets going once the world has been populated with lots and lots of people. Remember all the sex people were having and all of the children? Well, it gets to the point where the whole world is full of people. And once it's full of people—earthlings, dirtbags—it is also necessarily full of violence. Because people know the difference between good and evil—but don't have the ability to always choose good over evil. So God takes a look around.

> The Lord saw that the wickedness of humankind was great in the earth, and that the entire will of the intentions of their hearts was only evil continually. And the Lord was sorry that he had made humankind on the earth, and it grieved

him to his heart. So the Lord said, "I will blot out from the earth the human beings I have created." (Genesis 6:5–7)

Now take this seriously. God, who had evaluated the beloved creation and found it to be balanced and good, looks at the way humanity lives. And God is sorry that God has made humanity—which at first was "very good."

You are reading these words long after I have written them, but my guess is that there is still a hell of a lot of violence going on. As I write, Venezuela and North Korea and Sudan are impossibly corrupt, and their people are enduring unbearable suffering. There might be war with North Korea, whose leader seems both insane and terrified—not a good combo. In Libya, black Africans are being enslaved and sold by north Africans. And so on. In my own country, this has been a year in which the unspeakable depth of an epidemic of sexual harassment, sexual abuse, and sexual assault has finally been spoken. And my country has been called by the #MeToo movement to address the corruption that is so deeply seated in our flesh. Locally, in my city we are struggling with the evil of sex-trafficking. Racism, sexism, a war on children (both born and unborn) are massive problems.

THE ELDER

I believe your forgot about the war on Christmas!

In summary: the earth is corrupt and full of violence. And the question is, What is a good and just God going to do about it?

The point of the flood story is that when God evaluates sin—the brokenness of creation, and especially the capacity in the human will for violence, evil, and bloodshed—God's sense of justice is so gravely offended that just for a brief moment, forty days and forty nights, God considers starting over. God's sense of justice is so aggrieved by the weakness and violence in our human flesh that God considers doing what any of us do when one of our creations turns out wrong—we toss it out, start over, and try again. When I bake a batch of cookies that don't turn out, I throw them away and start over. When I write a chapter for a book or an article for a journal and it isn't going well, I start over.

In light of sin, God considers starting over. But God doesn't. Noah pleases God. And because of Noah, God preserves humanity.

Part of the good news here is that God is a God of justice. Because God loves all of creation, when any part of creation suffers, God's sense of justice is triggered. God doesn't look at the evil humans do and just shrug and go, "No big deal. Works for me." It doesn't work for God. God's sense of justice is so finely tuned that violence and oppression deeply grieve God. Illness and disability deeply grieve God. God is so grieved by our violence that God was a moment away from just starting over. That is how much God cares about justice. Because God is a God of love, when the beloved creation goes wrong, the loving God's very heart breaks.

THE DEACON

The God of the flood seems too much like me in middle school playing video games. If I was losing to my little brother, I would get a sudden leg spasm and hit the reset button on the Nintendo.

But there's more. God is love. And in addition to justice, God is also a God of mercy. God doesn't kill Cain when Cain slays his brother. God banishes him and gives him a blessing. God considers starting over, but then the story says that God sees Noah. And "Noah found favor in the sight of the Lord." Something about Noah triggers the mercy side of God's love. There may be few lines in the Bible as tender and wonderful as that: "Noah found favor in the sight of the Lord." God looks at Noah. God loves. And so, instead of destroying the creation and starting over, God resolves to find a different way—other than more violence and more bloodshed—to deal with the corruption of the human will and of all flesh.

So Noah downloads God's plans for a big ark. It isn't really a ship. It's more of a box. Noah isn't a sea captain but someone who really trusts God. Noah and his wife, their three sons and their wives, and two of every kind of animal crawl into the ark, and the rains come down.

There are many cool details in the flood story, but perhaps the coolest is how after the whole earth is filled with

Why didn't Noah go fishing from the ark? He only had two worms.

THE DEACON

water, Noah sends out a raven and a dove to see if there is dry land anywhere. Finally, one day the dove returns with an olive branch in its beak—and ever since, both the dove and the olive branch have been symbols of peace. When one warring party "extends the olive branch" to another, it is an offer of peace. The olive branch that the dove brings back is the promise of peace from God.

The First Covenant

The waters recede, the ark hits dry land, all the passengers pile out. The first thing that Noah does is worship God. He builds an altar and offers up a sacrifice. Then the Lord makes a promise—a covenantal promise. God says, "Look, I know that the entire will of the human heart is evil from youth. But I will never again set out to start over by destroying all flesh. So go, have a lot of sex and a lot of kids. Fill the earth. But do not murder each other. For every human being is created in my image."

Then, as part of the covenant, God puts the rainbow in the sky and promises, "This is the sign of the covenant that I make between me and you and every living creature that is with you, for all future generations: I have set my rainbow in the clouds, and it shall be a sign of the covenant between me and the earth. . . . When the rainbow is in the clouds, I will see it and remember the everlasting covenant between God and every living creature of all flesh that is on the earth."

This is the first covenant in the Bible. Every covenant has partners, a promise, and a sign. Here, God and "every living creature" are the partners. The promise is that God will not set out to destroy all life and start over. And the sign is the rainbow, which God puts in the sky not to remind us of the promise but to remind God that God made the promise.

And then? Well, then Noah gets drunk and passes out naked. His son Ham comes in and something happens. The text isn't quite clear. Elsewhere in the Bible, the euphemism "uncover the nakedness of" can mean to have sex with (see Leviticus 18). That phrase isn't exactly used in Genesis 9. Here it says that Ham "saw the nakedness of his father." For this crime, Ham and his descendants (the Canaanites) are cursed and ordered to be slaves to Shem and his descendants. What's the point of this story? The main point is that human brokenness was not drowned in the flood. There is beauty and there is ugliness in the human heart. The first two things Noah does after disembarking from the floating box are worship God and then pass out drunk and naked. Sin persists—God will find another way of dealing with sin, other than through more violence.

But notice the pattern: Sin (human violence) → Consequence (flood) → Blessing (covenant).

The Tower of Babel

Israel's prehistory concludes with a story known as the Tower of Babel, in which the people of the east intend to build a city "with a tower with its head in the heavens, and let us make a name for ourselves; otherwise we shall be scattered broad over the face of the earth" (Genesis 11:4). Ironically, the very thing that the people fear is the exact punishment the Lord chooses for their pride. "The Lord confused the language of the earth; and from there the Lord scattered them abroad across the face of the earth" (11:9).

For the purposes of this book, I only want to draw attention to the curious detail that once again we see the pattern of a people committing a sin. Again, the sin is a version of not staying in their lane—they want to make a name for themselves and build a tower to the heavens. And the Lord judges the sin and there is a consequence—human languages are confused, and the people are scattered.

But this time, there's no blessing.

What Kind of Literature Is This?

Genres of literature are sets of conventions through which producers of literature communicate with their audiences. Someone who writes an editorial in the newspaper is trying to get an opinion across. Someone who tells a joke at the start of a speech is trying to relax the audience and gain their attention. Someone who writes a news account of an important event is trying to describe key aspects of the event as accurately as possible.

What is Genesis 1–11? Many people have insisted that we must read these chapters as history—as historically accurate accounts of how things happened. But compelling reasons exist to conclude that the people who produced this literature did not think of themselves as writing history. The story includes a talking snake, fruit that imparts knowledge of good and evil once eaten, people who live to extraordinarily old ages, a great flood that fills the entire earth, two animals of every species fitting into one ark (what about the bison and musk oxen in North America?), and the idea that only three people are alive, yet when Cain is banished he fears that someone might kill him, and when he departs, he "knows" his wife (where did she come from?), and then they build a city (where did the people to populate the city come from)? The people who produced this literature were not bothered by these questions—most likely because they didn't imagine that they were producing history, and therefore they weren't worried that anyone would ask those sorts of questions.

This literature is best described as theological parables. Just as Jesus told parables such as the Good Samaritan, the Prodigal Son, or the Sheep and the Goats, the authors of these stories were telling theological parables— which some people have described as stories with spiritual meaning. Both Judaism and Christianity have regarded these stories as inspired by God's Spirit—meaning that the truths these stories disclose are authoritative for how we understand God, ourselves, and the creation.

3

Blessed to Be a Blessing, and Other Terrifying Thoughts

Following the story of the tower of Babel and the ensuing scattering of the nations and confusing of languages, there ensues a passage that contains more people having sex and children and yet another genealogy, this one tracing the descendants of Shem. As the descendants are traced, we finally hear about some people whose names later because famous:

> Now these are the descendants of Terah. Terah was the father of Abram, Nahor, and Haran; and Haran was the father of Lot. Haran died before his father Terah in the land of his birth, in Ur of the Chaldeans. Abram and Nahor took wives; the name of Abram's wife was Sarai, and the name of Nahor's wife was Milcah. She was the daughter of Haran the father of Milcah and

Iscah. Now Sarai was barren; she had no child.
(Genesis 11:27–30)

A new word occurs here that hasn't appeared yet in the
Bible, a theologically and economically profound word:
barren. We read, "Now Sarai was barren; she had no
child." The Bible's full of knowing, conceiving, and giving birth to, without interruption. Until Sarai. "Sarai was
barren; she had no child."

So now we have two problems.

The first problem has been caused by God, and it's a
problem on a global scale. God has scattered the nations
and confused their languages. We already know that "the
entire will of the hearts of human beings is constantly evil"
(Genesis 6:5). And now we have a world where people are
different from each other ethnically; in addition, the different nations might not understand each other because of
the confusion of languages.

THE ELDER

I imagine pre-Babel
humanity to be on par
with the comment
section on YouTube.

The second problem is Sarai's barrenness. Not a
global problem, rather, it's a problem that many families,
couples, and individuals have every day, everywhere,
every when. As the first person in the uninterrupted list of
knowing, conceiving, and bearing who is barren, Sarai

stands out. Is her barrenness a sign of a curse? Maybe a curse from God? The world tends to think in this way. Later in the Bible there are women who are barren, and the narrator of the story will comment, "because the Lord had closed her womb." Or some other such conclusion. This is just how the world tends to think. When something goes wrong, some people will say, "Everything happens for a reason. God don't make no mistakes." Thus, according to the way that the world thinks, some would certainly have wondered about Sarai, "Is the Lord punishing her?" Why would people wonder such a thing? Well, remember sin? Yeah, people suck sometimes.

Issues concerning women's bodies and fertility remain difficult for communities of

THE BISHOP

faith. Too many struggle with infertility and miscarriages alone. We need to break the silence.

But Sarai's problem is not just a problem for her. It's also a problem for her husband, Abram. Because Sarai is barren, Abram's future is clouded. Ancient society was built upon a *kinship society*. In the ancient world, your extended family was your social safety net, its welfare was your purpose in life, it was the group of people in which you formed your identity and lived your life.

An aside: in the 1970s, my father went on an archaeo-logical dig in Israel. While he was there, he got to visiting with a Palestinian man. They exchanged stories and asked each other questions about life, family, and the like. At one point my dad asked him, "Do you have any social-security system for when you get old?" The man said, "My sons are my social security." Meaning, of course, that when people get old, they have their children and grandchildren to take care of them. That's how a kinship society works: your family is your social-security system, your social safety net, and it is your duty to serve the family.

The Old Testament has four levels of kinship:

People or Kindred—At the highest level, you were a member of a *people* (Hebrew: *'am*), also called a *kindred* (*moledeth*). This highest level was probably ruled by a king or queen, or later a governor. In the Old Testament, the name of the people was the Hebrews, or Israel, or Judah (but also Ephraim or Jacob after the people split into two nations in 922 BCE).

Tribe—The second-highest level of the people's kin-ship society was the *tribe* (Hebrew: *matteh*). Israel gener-ally had twelve tribes.

Clan—The third-highest level of the society was the *clan* (Hebrew: *mishpachah*). The clans generally were sets of extended families. The clans could get very large. And it seems to be the case that when a tribe diminished over time, a large clan might rise up to take its place. That explains why the lists of tribes in the Old Testament are not always completely identical.

Father's House—The lowest level of the society was the *father's house* (Hebrew: *bet-'av*). This was literally a three-story house in which a grandfather and grandmother (called the *father* and *mother* of the house) lived with their adult children (until they formed their own houses) and with some of their grandchildren.

And all of this kinship society existed in a place, in a given land, and to leave a land meant leaving your kinship society.

The Call of and Four Promises to Abram and Sarai

Abram and Sarai are ready to be their own *father's house*—but they can't, because they have no kids. Then this happens:

> Terah took his son Abram and his grandson Lot son of Haran, and his daughter-in-law Sarai, his son Abram's wife, and they went out together from Ur of the Chaldeans to go into the land of Canaan; but when they came to Haran, they settled there. The days of Terah were two hundred five years; and Terah died in Haran (Genesis 11:31–32).

Notice that Abram's father, Terah, has moved his father's house from their land, Ur of the Chaldeans—a city in the southeastern part of the Mesopotamian valley—and they settle in Haran—a city in the northwestern part of the Mesopotamian valley. But then Terah dies, leaving Abram and Sarai to lead a family unit that includes their nephew Lot—but no other kids, no kids of their own. So a father's house with no house, so to speak.

So now, let's put all three of these things together. First, God needs to come up with some kind of blessing to deal with the scattering of the nations. Second, Sarai is barren—which may have meant that some people would have assumed she wasn't favored by the gods or God. Third, Abram and Sarai have moved and are now an isolated father's house, far from their land.

THE ACOLYTE

Oh junk! I just got what you are putting down. The biblical narrative is one where God transforms the challenges and conundrums humanity brings creatively into a blessing. God is the blessing-ator.

THE DEACON

I dig it, Acolyte! God isn't a Terminator but a Blessing-ator.

THE BISHOP

Don't tell Rolf or he will make a Bacon-ator joke.

And into this mess, God appears to Abram with a call and some promises:

> Now the Lord said to Abram, "Go from your land and your kindred and your father's house to the land that I will show you. I will make of you a great nation, and I will bless you, and make your name great, so that you will be a blessing. I will bless those who bless you, and the one who curses you I will curse; and in you all the clans of the earth shall be blessed." (Genesis 12:1–3)

There's much to unpack here, but let's start with the shocking, even ridiculous, nature of God's actions. God needs to find a way to create a permanent blessing to address the scattering of the human race into many peoples and tribes. So naturally God chooses Abram and Sarai to be the blessing for the nations. Oh, and in the next verse we find out that Abram is old: "Abram was seventy-five years old." Later, we find out that Sarah is ten years younger than Abram.

What kind of counterintuitive, cray-cray, ludicrous decision is that? God chooses a childless couple, seventy-five and sixty-five years old, to be the family through which "all the clans of the earth shall be blessed"?

And Abram and Sarai—rather than going back to his own kindred (the highest level of kinship), land (location of the kinship group), and father's house (the lowest level of his kinship group)—say yes to God, the "Let It Be" moment of the Old Testament. In the New Testament, the key necessary for the saving drama of Jesus Christ to get rolling is Mary agreeing to become an unwed, virgin mother, pregnant with a child of the Holy Spirit. Abram and Sarai saying yes to becoming sojourners or aliens—that is, people who are separated from their kinship systems—is akin to the Mary moment.

Interpreters have focused on both the call of Abram and Sarai and also on the promises that God offered. In truth, there is not an explicit *call* moment in these three verses. Abram is not asked if he will follow God, nor is he given the explicit opportunity to say no. But the choice is implied, so many readers have found it helpful to title these verses the call of Abram. But more important in this passage are the promises made to Abram.

1. *Land*—God commands the couple to go "to the land that I will show you." This is critical, because a kinship group needed a place, a land in which to be.

2. *Descendants and Great Nation*—God promises, "I will make of you a great nation." From the humble beginnings of two elderly sojourners, God promises that their descendants will eventually become a great nation. Scholars usually call this promise *progeny* ('cuz that's a word people use every day), but I prefer *descendants*, simply because it's more understandable. But notice the emphasis on the nation—Abram and Sarai's descendants will become an entire kinship group, rising from a childless father's house to become a nation.

3. *Great Name*—Earlier, in the tower of Babel story, the people desire to "make a name for ourselves," lest they be scattered. The one people are, ironically, scattered. And now, even more ironically, the

people God is choosing in order to bless the many
scattered nations will themselves be given "a great
name."

4. *Blessing to Be a Blessing*—The most important, by
far, of the four promises is the promise that they
will receive a blessing from God. "I will bless
you . . . so that you will be a blessing. I will bless
those who bless you, and the one who curses you I
will curse; and in you all the clans of the earth shall
be blessed" (Genesis 12:2–3). The people are to be
"a priestly kingdom" (Exodus 19:6).

Does this seem fair to you, that God chooses one nation to
be a priestly nation, "blessed to be a blessing?" No. It isn't
fair. God's choice of Abram and Sarai—the technical term
is God's *election of Israel*—isn't fair. As my friend police
officer Mike says, "The fair is in August, it's where they
judge pigs."

But who says God's grace is fair? God threw fair out of
the equation when God decided not to destroy the world
because of sin and start over. If God's actions were about
fair, the waters would never have receded from the flood
and God's people would have gills and mer-people tails.
So don't ask for fair. God chooses Abram and Sarai—an
old couple with no kids. Why? Maybe because no other
people would say yes. Maybe no other couple wanted to
leave home and trust God. Maybe it was because Abram
and Sarai were such unlikely candidates to become great.
No kids. And, as we'll see shortly, not always the best-
quality people.

And maybe being God's chosen people isn't all it's
cracked up to be. Sort of like being the one kid that Mom

asks to take out the trash, being chosen of God isn't always a picnic. Being chosen means God has higher standards for them than for others. And being chosen by God means other nations will hate on Israel over and over again. As Tevye says to God in *Fiddler on the Roof*, "We are the Chosen People. But, once in a while, can't You choose someone else?"[1]

The choice or *election* of Israel to be God's blessed-to-be-a-blessing, priestly nation is the scandal of the Old Testament. From a human point of view, it makes no sense—no human being could come up with it. The same for God's choice of one nation—especially *a nation descended from this couple*—it makes no sense—no human being could come up with it. And that is the point.

THE DEACON

I like the idea that after Babel, God knew better than to try to relate to everyone the same way and instead chose to invest in a particular people for the blessing of all.

God's Endangered Promises—The Plot of Genesis through Joshua

God's four promises to Abram and Sarai supply the plot for the rest of Genesis, the plot for the rest of Pentateuch, and the plot from Genesis 12 all the way through to the end of the book of Joshua.

Over and over again in Genesis through Joshua, one or more of God's four promises to Abram and Sarai becomes endangered. And—SPOILER ALERT!—over and over again, God finds a way to keep the promises. Indeed, the main theological affirmation of Genesis through 2 Kings is that *God is faithful to God's promises. God keeps God's promises.* Very often, humans do various things—sometimes faithless things, sometimes foolish things, and somethings just frail-ish things—to endanger God's promises. And still, over and over again, God comes through.

CHAPTER 3, OPTIONAL QUEST #1: READ GENESIS 12:1–25:11 (COMPLETE QUEST AND LEVEL UP TO PENTATEUCH NERD, LEVEL 1).

The Abraham, Sarah, and Hagar Story

As soon as Abram arrives in the promised land, he builds an altar to worship the Lord. Immediately, there is a famine. So Abram—great man of faith that he is—flees to Egypt. On the way, he says to Sarai, "Hey, you're hot for a seventy-year-old. When we get there, we'll tell everyone you're my sister—otherwise they might kill me." And thus it is that as soon as they reach Egypt, Sarai is taken in Pharaoh's harem.

So, just fifteen verses into the story, the promises are already endangered by Abram's foolish and faithless actions. They aren't in the land, and there aren't any heirs yet.

To get the promises back on track, the Lord curses Egypt. Pharaoh's house experiences "great plagues." When Pharaoh realizes that Sarai is Abram's wife, he packs them both on their way, with lots of good gifts for the journey.

THE ELDER

Ole Abe gets pretty close to pimpin' his wife. By close, I mean it would be uncomfortable to call Abe a pimp, so I stick with close.

Many years go by, and Abram and Sarai remain childless. Thus the promises are endangered—this time by Abram and Sarai's childlessness. The Lord speaks again to Abram. "Trust me, I am your shield." But Abram laments, "I'm still childless. You have not given me a child! My servant Eliezer is my heir!" It is nighttime. "Go outside, Abram. Count the stars if you are able. THAT is how many descendants you and Sarai will have."

"But how do I know that will actually happen?" asks Abram.

Then the Lord makes Abram a solemn oath—and enters into a covenant with Abram. God decides to amp up the relationship with Abram to the level of a covenant. And this covenant—the Abrahamic covenant—is the second covenant in the Old Testament (the covenant with Noah is first). God does some cool ritual things with a cow, a goat, a ram, a turtledove, a pigeon, a smoking pot of fire, and an autonomous torch. Then God renews the divine promises to Abram and Sarai.

Having been given to Pharaoh by Abram down in Egypt, Sarai has learned a thing or two about throwing someone who trusts you under the bus. So Sarai, hurting for her husband who has no child yet, gives someone who trusts her to Abram—to have sex with and thus to have a child. Sarai makes Hagar—her Egyptian slave, whom we must assume she acquired from Pharaoh—have sex with Abram. And Hagar gets pregnant. A teacher of mine once pointed out in a lecture to a room full of young seminary students that Genesis 16 doesn't say whether Hagar thought this was a good idea. "But let me ask the women present a question," Katharine Doob Sakenfeld posed, "Do any of you want to have sex with a ninety-year-old tonight?"

I can hear the silence.

THE ACOLYTE

Another of my teachers, Diane Jacobson, has said that we can consider this passage the first sex-trafficking in the Bible. And it was Sarai who traffics Hagar to Abram. After Hagar gets pregnant, Sarai starts to treat her unjustly. Hagar runs away. But God appears to her and says, "You shall name your son, Ishmael [which means *God has heard*], because the Lord has heard your pain" (Genesis 16:11).

So Abram has a son with Hagar, named Ishmael, but Sarai remains childless. When Abram turns ninety-nine, with Sarai eighty-nine, God speaks again to Abram and says, "I am again renewing my promise to you."

Abram laughs at God. He laughs so hard that he falls on his face. The gut-wrenching, soul-crushing laughter of unbelief. Did I mention? He is ninety-nine.

"No really," God says. "And to prove it, I am changing your name to Abraham [which means *father of many*], for your descendants will be many. This is a covenant— and the sign of the covenant shall be male circumcision." Talk about cutting a deal with God! [Rimshot]. God continues, "And your wife's name will be Sarah, because I will bless her and give her a son."

THE DEACON

He said "rimshot" about a circumcision joke. :)

And then Abraham says one of the most tragic and loving, but also one of the most clueless and loveless, things in the Bible. In response to God renewing the covenant and including Sarah, Abraham prays, "O that Ishmael might live in your sight!" This is a sad and loving prayer because Abraham loves Ishmael and wants him to be a child of God, too. But this is also a clueless prayer, because of Sarah! God is including Sarah in the covenant and in the promises!

So God responds, "Dude, she's your wife! This isn't just about you, you know. This is about *Sarah* and *Sarah's* son-to-be! But regarding Ishmael, there are promises for him, too. I will bless him; I will make his descendants a great nation; he shall be the father of twelve princes; but the covenant will go through Sarah's son." Notice that—the covenant goes through Sarah. But still, they have to wait.

One really hot day, when Abraham is chilling in his tent, he looks up and sees three strangers. He runs out and welcomes them. He gets the best flour, the best meat, the best milk and cheese—and he personally serves them. "Where's Sarah?" they ask. "In the tent." Then one says, "I'll be back in nine months and Sarah will be holding a son."

And Sarah laughs. The expletive-deleted sort of laugh that comes from the bottom of a broken heart. And Sarah says, "I'm old and way past the time of childbearing—I haven't had my period in thirty years! And Abraham, he's so old he can't even give me pleasure any more, if you get what I'm sending."

And nine months later, Isaac is born. Isaac, whose name means *he laughs*. Who laughs? Maybe God laughs. God laughs when God keeps God's promises.

Then God does a terrible thing. Or at least it seems that way to me. Maybe God had a good reason. I don't know. God puts Abraham to the test.

Many Christians say the Lord's Prayer weekly or daily. One of the lines in the Lord's Prayer goes like this: "Do not bring us to the time of testing" or "save me from the time of trial." (Both of which are more faithful translations than "Do not lead us into temptation.") If you want to know what "do not bring us to the time of testing" means, Genesis 22 is the place to start.

The text starts out, "After these things God tested Abraham." After what things? After Abraham followed

THE ELDER

I also find Olive Garden's unlimited soup, salad, and breadstick meal to be a genuine temptation it's best I avoid.

God and waited and waited for a child. After years of heartbreak. After Ishmael was born and then sent away. After Isaac was born. After all of that, "God tested Abraham." God says to Abraham, "Take your son, your only son Isaac, whom you love, and go to the land of Moriah, and offer him there as a burnt offering on one of the mountains that I shall show you."

Why? Why now? Why test Abraham at all? And why test Abraham in this horrible way? There is no way to know, because the text doesn't tell us. But in order to understand the text, we probably have to ditch conventional notions regarding God's omniscience. Some people believe that God knows all—including that God knows the future perfectly. This text seems to indicate that such a view of God's omniscience comes from some source other than the Old Testament. Here, at the very least, God always knows what God is going to do—God all along intends not to let Abraham actually kill Isaac. But God does not know what Abraham will do.

Abraham obeys God. He brings Isaac to the mountain God shows him. Abraham carries the fire and the knife. Isaac carries the wood. Isaac asks his father—whose name means Father-of-Many—"Father, where is the lamb for the offering?" "God will provide," Father-of-Many replies. When they reach the mountain, Abraham binds Isaac and prepares to sacrifice the boy, but God stops him. "Now I know that you fear God." Abraham looks up and sees a ram stuck in a bush. The story ends well for everyone except the ram, which Abraham sacrifices instead of his son.

What is the meaning of such a story? First, the story is a promise. God will provide. God will find a way to keep God's promises—even when it seems that God is the one who is endangering the promises. Second, the story is a law. Many of Israel's neighbors practiced child sacrifice. Some within Israel, including some later kings who were influenced by their neighbors but also out of their own superstition, also committed child sacrifice. The story communicates that God's people are not to engage in child sacrifice. A nice goat is plenty for a sacrifice. Third, the story is a story about letting go of one's own desires and submitting to God. Abraham submits to God; Isaac submits to his father, Abraham. There are times in life when we must let go of our own desires and trust God's guidance. Fourth, when you pray that God will not "bring us to the time of trial"— really mean that prayer. I would not have passed the test God gave Abraham. Nope. No way. Fifth, notice again that Israel's God is not some God who hangs out at a distance, content to remain indifferent to life in the good-but-broken creation. God really got right up into Abraham's grill. God was so committed to the relationship that God made sure that God knew Abraham really feared God. Sixth, this story is terrifying, and there's no explanation for it.

For the record, God and Abraham never speak again. Some tests, apparently, don't leave the tester and the testee on speaking terms afterward.

THE BISHOP

Sarah never talks to
Abraham again either.
I don't blame either one
of them.

But God finds a way to keep the promise. God always does.

After some years pass, Sarah dies. Abraham remarries and has six more sons by his new wife, Keturah. Why do I mention this? Just as another reminder that this story is as much about God's fidelity to Sarah as to Abraham. Abraham had eight sons by three women—but this story is just as much about Sarah as it is about Abraham. This story is really, really, really about Sarah.

After seeing that Isaac is properly married off to a member of his own people (not some gum-snapping Canaanite woman), Abraham also dies. Ishmael comes back and joins Isaac to bury their father next to Sarah.

Abraham and Sarah were buried in the land that the Lord had promised them—you can visit their graves to this day.

The Jacob Story (Featuring Esau, Laban, Leah, Rachel, Dinah, and More)

CHAPTER 3, OPTIONAL QUEST #2: READ GENESIS 26–32 (COMPLETE QUEST AND LEVEL UP TO PENTATEUCH NERD, LEVEL 2).

If the issue for Abraham and Sarah was that they didn't have a son—the issue for Isaac and Rebekah is *which* son, because they have twin boys—Esau and Jacob.

Here's the thing you need to know about Jacob: He's a wrestler. Even while he is in the womb with his brother, he's wrestling. Striving to outdo his brother, to be king of the hill, or rather, king of the womb. The two boys struggle so fiercely within their mother that Rebekah wonders, "If it has to be this way, why am I even alive?" Esau is born first. But ever the grappler, Jacob comes out right after his brother—grasping Esau's heel firmly in his little newborn hand.

Some brothers have friendly rivalries. That isn't the case with Jacob and Esau. They are very different. Esau is a hunter, preferring to spend time in the fields. He's daddy's favorite. He gets his deer on opening weekend and goes fishing with Dad. Jacob is quiet, preferring to hang out around the home place and learning how to cook. He's a momma's boy, Rebekah's favorite.

THE ELDER

For the nonhunters, *opening weekend* refers to the first week of hunting season. When those hardcore hunters like Esau "get their deer," it means they got all of their tagged kills for the season. The number is based on the population of deer who lack predators other than cars and food in the suburbs.

THE ACOLYTE

So shooting deer means less wolves, wrecks, and starving deer. . . . I still don't like shooting Bambi.

By virtue of being born a few seconds ahead of Jacob, Esau has two things that his younger brother wants. The first is what was known as the birthright. With the birthright came a double share of the inheritance. When the inheritance was sorted out, they would take the number of sons (here two) and add one share (2 + 1 = 3), and the oldest would get an extra share. That means two for Esau and one for Jacob. The second thing that Esau has coming is the blessing. As in the blessed-to-be-a-blessing blessing from God.

One day, when Esau returns from the hunt so famished that he thinks he's going to die, Jacob trades him a bowl of chili for Esau's birthright. Esau's logic is simple, "If I die, the birthright is no good to me." Jacob's logic is simple greed. He covets his brother's birthright. So, instead of showing the hospitality that he owes his brother (and that Abraham had shown to complete strangers), Jacob takes advantage of his brother's need.

But it gets worse. Because after he gets his grasping hands on the birthright, he sets his sight on Esau's blessing. But to wrestle the blessing away from Esau, he calls in some help: his mother, Rebekah. By the time Isaac is ready to pass the blessing on to the next generation, he's old. Too many years in the desert sun have left his eyes clouded over with cataracts. Isaac sends Esau out on the hunt with the intention of blessing Esau after they have enjoyed a feast. But Rebekah overhears, so as soon as Esau is gone, she sends Jacob out to the barn to kill a couple of goats. While she cooks the stew, Jacob disguises himself as Esau. Then Rebekah sends Jacob in to get the blessing: "I am Esau, your firstborn; sit up, eat, and bless me." Isaac almost sniffs out the fraud. "The voice is the voice of Jacob," he says. But the disguise holds up. "Are you really Esau?" "Yep," lies Jacob. And so Isaac blesses Jacob—who tricks his father with the help of his mother.

It's pretty clear at this point being blessed by God doesn't fix some seriously screwed up family dynamics.

THE BISHOP

When Esau returns and comes in for the blessing, it is a scene of great sadness. Isaac realizes that his very own son tricked him and lied to him. Esau pleads, "Have you only one blessing to give, father? Bless me also!" Isaac does what he can for Esau, but there is only one blessing. Isaac weeps. But Esau rages and plans to kill Jacob. It's Cain and Abel all over again.

Thus, the story of Isaac ends with the promises endangered anew. Jacob has to flee, so he is not in the promise. In addition, he has no wife—so the promise of descendants and a great nation are unfulfilled at Isaac's death. And there is the difficult matter of Jacob having twice cheated his brother Esau. How would God react to a blessing on a cheater, a grappler, a heel?

On the first day of his escape, when darkness falls and Jacob can travel no farther, he lays down to sleep with nothing but a rock for a pillow. And there—in the middle of the night, in the middle of nowhere, with his head on a rock—God does what God is pleased to do. God shows up. God shows up in the middle of Jacob's self-induced suffering.

With the dulcet lyre-tones of Led Zeppelin supplying the soundtrack, Jacob has a vision of a stairway to heaven in his dream. And on the stairway, he sees the angels of God going up and coming down. And then the Lord is right there next to him, making promises: "I am the Lord, the God of Abraham and Isaac. I am here to reaffirm the promise of the covenant. I promise you this land to you and your descendants. Your descendants will be as numerous as the dust of the earth. I will bless you and all the clans of the earth shall be blessed through you. And I will be with you" (Genesis 28:13–15).

Jacob wakes up from his dream and says, "Surely the Lord is in this place and I didn't even know it!"

So where does God show up in Jacob's story? First, God shows up out in the world. Not in worship—although God is there, too. But note that God shows up in daily life—"Surely the Lord is in this place and I didn't even know," Jacob realizes. Second, God shows up when and where Jacob is hurting—in his pain and suffering. Sure, Jacob has caused his own pain and suffering by sinning against his brother. But just because he made his own bed doesn't mean it isn't a sucky place to be. His pain is both quite genuine and also genuinely painful. But God shows up—renewing the promises.

That will preach.

THE BISHOP

There is not enough space in this book to go into the rest of Jacob's story in detail. But it's more of the same. Jacob spends time working for his Uncle Laban, who turns a fast one on Jacob—tricking the trickster. Jacob marries Laban's daughters Leah and Rachel. And Jacob keeps wrestling with his circumstances. God's promises keep being endangered. God keeps finding ways to keep the promises.

When it comes time for Jacob to return to the promised land, Abraham's grandson is well on the way to becoming a great nation. Jacob ends up having a whole load of children with Leah and her servant Zilpah, as well as with Rachel and her servant Bilhah. In all, Jacob has twelve sons—these sons become the ancestors of the twelve tribes of Israel. The most well-known of the sons are probably Judah (the ancestor of the Southern Kingdom), Levi (the ancestor of the tribe of priests), and Joseph (whose story is told in Genesis 37–50). Jacob also has a number of daughters, including Dinah—whose tragic story of redemption from sexual exploitation is told in Genesis 34.

God keeps the promise of blessed-to-be-a-blessing—through Jacob's blessing, Laban grows exceedingly wealthy. Jacob also prospers in Laban's service, but God tells him it is time for the promise of the land to be kept. So Jacob departs Laban's service and points his large caravan of people and livestock toward the land.

As Jacob nears the land, word reaches him that his brother Esau is coming out to greet him—along with four hundred armed men. The Bible says, "Then Jacob was greatly afraid and distressed" (Genesis 32:7). Yeah, right. He probably needed to change his pants. The old manipulator thinks himself a typical, manipulative thought. "I'll divide my caravan in two. If Esau captures one, I'll still have half my wealth." In fact, he sends half of his wealth on ahead to his brother as a, umm, gift? Bribe? Payback? All of the above? And Jacob prays. Oh, how he prays to be delivered from the righteous anger of his brother!

That night, God shows up. And the old wrestler has the match of his life. All night long, Jacob wrestles with God. Finally, Jacob's opponent kicks him in the hip and says, "Allow me to go." "I won't let you go until you bless me!" Jacob demands. Not only does God bless Jacob, but God changes Jacob's name to Israel, "for you have wrestled with God and prevailed." Jacob limps for the rest of his life. But the new man—Israel—knows for the rest of his life that God has blessed him. Remember that "great name" that God promised Abraham and Sarah? Here it is: "Israel: one who struggles with God and prevails." That's a pretty cool name.

And Esau? He isn't there to seek revenge but to achieve reconciliation. Blessing indeed.

The Joseph Story—When There Are Too Many Brothers

CHAPTER 3, OPTIONAL QUEST #3: READ GENESIS 37–50 (COMPLETE QUEST AND LEVEL UP TO PENTATEUCH NERD, LEVEL 3).

Genesis 37–50 recounts the story of Jacob's eleventh son, Joseph. As you no doubt know, family dysfunction in one generation tends to work its way into the lives of the next generation and the next generation. So let's review the chosen family's function to date. Abraham lets his wife go to Pharaoh's harem and lets his son Ishmael be sent away. Isaac is almost sacrificed by his own father. Jacob and his mother, Rebekah, trick Isaac and steal Esau's blessing. It probably won't come as a shocker that the family dysfunction continues. Joseph is the first son of Jacob's favorite wife Rachel, and he is also a "child of Jacob's old age." So Jacob favors Joseph. He gives him special gifts—including a rocking cloak. Maybe it was a coat of many colors. Maybe it was a sparkling coat with Elvis-style rhinestones and sequins.

Why was the "coat of many colors" such a big deal? Well, for one, every garment in the ancient world was made by hand. There was no mass production. You couldn't just go buy a coat at the nearest Target. An item of clothing was often the most expensive possession a person owned. In addition, clothing often could signal social status. Imagine you are one of ten older brothers—and your dad gives an incredibly audacious coat to your little snot brother. Did I mention once that Jacob sent Joseph to spy and report on his older brothers?

To top that off, God seems to favor Joseph, too. God sends Joseph special dreams and the ability to interpret dreams. In one dream, he and his brothers are twelve harvested bundles of grain—and the other eleven bundles bow down to him. In another dream, the sun, moon, and eleven stars bow down to his star.

THE ELDER

I am pretty sure God gives this dream to all younger brothers. I know mine had it, along with my youngest son.

If the issue with Abraham and Sarah was no child, and the issue with Isaac and Rebekah was which child, then the issue with Jacob and his wives is that there are too many children. With a favored little jerk like Joseph for a younger brother, this thing didn't seem headed toward a good ending. Then, in one of the vilest acts of betrayal since—well, since Jacob betrayed Esau—the ten older brothers sell Joseph into slavery in Egypt. They strip him of the hated coat of many colors, dunk the thing in blood, and bring the clothing home as a piece of false evidence. They show it to Jacob and say Joseph must have died. The brothers get rid of Joseph, but dad just picks a new favorite son—the twelfth son, Benjamin.

This family has all the makings of an excellent reality show. Joseph was the Kim Kardashian of the tribe.

THE ACOLYTE

The long story of Joseph is worth studying in detail—here there is only space for a brief overview. Spoiler alert: God finds a way to keep promises, which are constantly endangered.

In Egypt, Joseph is sold to a man named Potiphar, "an officer of Pharaoh, the captain of his guard" (Genesis 39:1). Let's get real for a minute. Joseph's life suddenly sucks. He has been the favorite son of a very wealthy man and also favored of God. Then, his very own brothers—the ones who should have shown him "loving faithfulness" (Hebrew: *chesed*, Israel's highest value)—betray him and sell him. And life in slavery sucks. It truly and really sucks.

But then the Bible says something mind-blowing. "The Lord was with Joseph, and he became a prosperous man. . . . The Lord made everything in his hand to prosper" (Genesis 39:2–3). Joseph rises until he is in charge of Potiphar's household. But his success draws the eye of Potiphar's wife. She wants a piece of Joseph. She lures him to the bedroom and grabs his cloak. Joseph refuses to have sex with her and flees the bedroom, leaving the cloak in her hand. When Potiphar gets home from guarding Pharaoh, she presents the piece of clothing as false evidence. She says that Joseph tried to rape her. Betrayed again, with the help of a little false evidence, Joseph finds himself in prison.

Let's get real again. Things sucked in slavery. But things really, really suck in prison. But guess what? "The Lord was with Joseph and showed Joseph loving faithfulness [Hebrew: *chesed*]. . . . The Lord was with him; and whatever he did, the Lord made to prosper" (Genesis 39:21–23). In prison, Joseph rises, and the warden entrusts many matters into Joseph's hand. Two of Pharaoh's lead servants—the palace sommelier and the head chef—end up in prison. One night they dream. Joseph is there to interpret the dreams for them. He tells the sommelier, "You have committed a minor penalty. You will sit in the penalty box for two minutes. You will feel shame. Then you go free. But promise me one thing. Promise that when you are pouring wine again for Pharaoh, you will remember me and show me loving faithfulness [Hebrew: *chesed*] and put in a good word for me."

"Oh, for sure! I won't forget you!" says the sommelier.

"What about me?" asks the chef.

"You have committed a major penalty and a game misconduct. It won't end well."

Pharaoh has the head chef hanged, but he frees the sommelier and restores him to his cushy job in the palace. Soon, he's pouring wine for Pharaoh by the pyramids. But the sommelier, far from showing Joseph loving faithfulness, forgets all about him.

Two years go by. And life in prison really, really sucks.

Then Pharaoh has a dream. He dreams that seven fat and healthy cows are grazing by the Nile River, when suddenly seven other cows—nasty and diseased—come and ate the healthy cows.

Long story short, the sommelier remembers this Hebrew in prison who could interpret dreams. Joseph is brought before the great man and explains, "You are about to have seven years of bumper crops and abundance, followed by seven years of famine and scarcity. Plan well, grasshopper. Put your best man in charge of the Royal Office of Planning and Economic Development."

"You are the man for the job, Joseph!" exclaims Pharaoh. Pharaoh puts Joseph in charge of the Royal Office of Planning and Economic Development. Joseph thinks about declining, but he remembers the head chef and feels *roped* into the job. [Rimshot.]

I believe this was also when the first tennis match in history took place . . . you know

THE DEACON

when Joseph *served* in Pharaoh's *court.*

The Bible does not say at this point that "the Lord was with Joseph and made everything he did to prosper." It doesn't have to say it. Because everything he did prospered. So when the great famine hits the ancient Near East, Pharaoh becomes wealthy and powerful beyond all reason.

Pharaoh gives Joseph a new name (Zaphenath-paneah) and marries him off to Asenath, the daughter of an important Egyptian priest. Joseph has two sons—Manasseh and Ephraim.

Guess Who's Coming to Dinner?

Meanwhile, back in the promised land, the famine hits pretty hard, and Joseph's family is soon on the edge of starvation. Jacob hears that there is food down in Egypt, so he sends down the older ten sons with instructions to buy some grain. But, since he has already lost one favorite son, he doesn't send Benjamin—the new favorite—with the ten. When the ten arrive in Egypt, they are sent in to bargain with some official named Zaphenath-paneah, husband of Asenath . . . whoever that is.

They don't recognize Joseph; a good sixteen years have gone by. But he recognizes them! And when they bow down to him, ooooooh does he ever remember his dreams!

Now ask yourself, what would you have done? These jack wagons sold you into slavery! In slavery, life sucked. And then it got worse. Life in prison sucked more. And whether he was with his brothers, or in slavery, or in prison, nobody ever showed Joseph the least bit of "loving faithfulness"—Israel's highest value.

Except God. All along, the Lord had shown Joseph constant loving faithfulness. And over time, that constant loving faithfulness changed Joseph. He is no longer the snotty little jerk who narced on his older brothers. He is no longer the full-of-himself narcissist who dreamed of having his brothers bow down to him. God's loving faithfulness—and life's ups and downs—have changed him over the years.

So Joseph says to his brothers, "It's me, Joseph. Don't worry! I'm not still mad. I know that you thought to do me evil. But through it all—in, with, and under all of the betrayal and lack of loving faithfulness—God has been at work to bring something good out of the evil. So, forgive and forget. If God has been at work to save our family and keep the divine promises, who am I to cancel God's good work? Go back home. Get dad. Tell him I'm alive. Tell him he's got a couple of more grandsons. Bring him down here and we'll get through this together."

And that is how Genesis ends. God is at work keeping the four-fold promises God made to Abraham and Sarah. The family is now a great clan, with many descendants. Through the family, God has been working to bless those who blessed them—including Laban and Pharaoh, of all people. The blessing is intact. In fact, Jacob's dying blessing goes to Joseph's boys, Manasseh and Ephraim.

When Jacob dies, Joseph brings his body up to the land of Canaan, so that like Abraham and Sarah, he can be buried in the land of the promise. But at the end of the book, the people are living in Egypt. So a part of the promise is as yet unkept.

The question is, "What will God do to keep the promise of the land, when the people are exiled in Egypt?"

From Pyramid to Promised Land: God's Free People (Exodus through Joshua)

The plot for the narrative arc that stretches from Genesis 12 through the end of the book of Jeremiah is supplied by the four promises that the Lord makes to Abraham in Genesis 12: the promises of a land, descendants that will become a great nation, a great name, and a blessing to be a blessing.

Let My People Go (Exodus 1–15)

CHAPTER 4, OPTIONAL QUEST #1: READ EXODUS 1–15 (COMPLETE QUEST AND LEVEL UP TO DELIVERANCE STAR, LEVEL 1).

At the close of Genesis, the promise of the blessing has been seen over and over again—through Abraham and Sarah's descendants, the Lord has been at work blessing the clans of the earth. Most spectacularly, Joseph's presence in Egypt has brought great blessings not only to Pharaoh but to the entire land. But the promise of the land is endangered, because as the last page is turned, the people are in Egypt. The opening words of Exodus invite us to make the connection to that reality: "These are the names of the sons of Jacob who came to Egypt with him" (1:1). The narrator adds, "Then Joseph died, and all his brothers, and that whole generation. But the Israelites were fruitful and prolific and they multiplied and grew exceedingly strong—until the land was filled with them" (1:6–7). In these verses, there's another connection to Genesis, with the allusion to God's command in Genesis 1 that the people be "fruitful and multiply and fill the land." Abraham and Sarah's descendants "filled the land"—but it was the wrong land.

Then comes one of the most ominous verses in the history of literature: "Now a new king arose over Egypt, who did not know Joseph" (1:8). The narrative does not explicitly say so, but many years have passed. During these years, the Israelites have grown numerous, but the "great name" of Joseph has diminished. Until, after many years, a new Pharaoh arises who doesn't know the story at all.

Because the new Pharaoh "did not know Joseph," he doesn't know this truth about God's work in the world: "I will bless those who bless you [the Israelites], and the one who curses you I will curse" (Genesis 12:3). The Pharaoh back in Genesis had blessed Joseph and shown Joseph "loving faithfulness." And things went well. The current

History has repeatedly
demonstrated how
deadly forgetting our
history can be.

THE BISHOP

Pharaoh in Egypt is about to step in the brown sticky-stinky big time. He is about to curse the Israelites. (Don't do it, don't do it!)

> The new Pharaoh said to his people, "The Israelites have become more numerous and more powerful than we. Let's do the smart thing, or they'll grow even more numerous and when war comes, they'll join our enemies to fight against us and escape from the land." Therefore they set taskmasters over them to oppress them with forced labor. . . . But the more they were oppressed, the more they multiplied and spread, until the Egyptians came to dread the Israelites. The Egyptians became ruthless in imposing tasks on the Israelites, and made their lives bitter with hard service in mortar and brick and in every kind of field labor. They were ruthless in all the tasks that they imposed on them. The king of Egypt said to the Hebrew midwives, the first was named Shiphrah and the second Puah, "When you act as midwives to the Hebrew women, and see them on the birthstool, if it is a boy, kill him; but if it is a girl, she shall live." (Exodus 1:9–16)

Ugh. Slavery again. Forced labor. Oppression. And now, genocide. Nice guy, that Pharaoh.

THE ACOLYTE

Luckily in America we would never freak out and act a fool when the historic people of privilege become a minority population. #Sarcasm

So what do the women do when Pharaoh commands them to murder all of the Israelite boys? They disobey. Why? "Because they feared God." Back in Genesis, Abraham and Joseph were said to "fear God." So in the God Fearers Hall of Fame, we've got Abraham, Joseph, Shiphrah, and Puah. To "fear God" is a hard concept to translate from Hebrew into English. If it were an equation, it could be drawn up like this:

being in awe of + loving + obeying × truly understanding = fearing God

Fearing God enables two women at the absolute bottom of the social-class ladder of ancient Egypt to stand up to the most powerful man on the continent. Amazing. I cannot possibly overemphasize this strongly enough. To be a slave, a woman, a foreigner,[1] and barren (see Exodus 1:21) was to be at the absolute bottom of society. Yet, that is exactly in this story where the reign of God is being born (no pun intended). (The bottom is always where the reign of God is being born—God's preferred future for the world comes into being in the midst of the hurts and suffering places on the planet. God works not from the top down but from the bottom up.)

Pharaoh isn't done trying to kill all the Hebrew boys: "Pharaoh commanded all his people, 'Every boy that is born to the Hebrews you shall throw into the Nile, but you shall let every girl live'" (Exodus 1:22). Once again, some women disobey Pharaoh. One Hebrew woman—from the tribe of Levi (more on that later)—hides a newborn son for three months. When she can hide him no longer, she weaves a papyrus *ark* (the same word as Noah's *ark*— another connection to the Genesis narrative) and, with her daughter, sets the boy afloat on the Nile River. Pharaoh's daughter, with a maid, finds the baby and decides to raise him as her own son, hiring the boy's very own mother to serve as his nurse. So notice again—Pharaoh's murderous intentions are spoiled by a handful of women—two Hebrews and two Egyptians. The reign of God breaking into the world from the underside and bubbling up.

One of the theological themes that is being worked out in this ancient conflict between The Man (Pharaoh) and this group of six women has to do with creation. Recall from chapter 2 that God's creative purposes are worked out, in part, as parts of the creation bring forth the next generation of creation. Plants produce seeds, which grow into the next generation of plants. Birds lay eggs, which hatch into the next generation of birds. And human beings are fruitful and multiply, filling the land, bringing God's creative will to bear and bringing forth the next generation of human beings.

Pharaoh, with his genocidal desire to murder the Hebrew boys and his dictatorial fear of the Hebrew people, is against God—against God's creative will and order. The Bible doesn't even honor Pharaoh by relating his name. As the Old Testament scholar Walter Brueggemann has joked, "You don't need to know his name. You've met one Pharaoh, you've met them all." But four of the women are named, so let's remember them for their fear of God, their choice of life, and God's creative order over death: Shiphrah, Puah, Jochebed (Moses's mother, see Exodus 6:20), and Miriam (Moses's sister, see Exodus 15:20). Let's also remember Pharaoh's daughter and her maid. May these women's stories be told and retold as long as stories are told.

THE ELDER

Can I get this story in a children's book for my granddaughter?

And the boy who is left to float down the River Nile in a papyrus ark? His name is Moses.

When Moses is grown, he sees an Egyptian slave master beating a Hebrew slave. He kills the Egyptian and hides the body. When word of Moses's crime gets around, he flees to the land of Midian. There he marries, has a son, and does his best to forget about Egypt.

But then the miraculous thing happens. "After a long time the king of Egypt died. The Israelites groaned under their slavery, and cried out. Out of the slavery their cry for help rose up to God. God heard their groaning, and God remembered the covenant with Abraham, Isaac, and Jacob. God looked upon the Israelites, and God took notice of them" (Exodus 2:23–25). Why did it take so long? God was waiting for Pharaoh to die. Why? See below.

God remembers the promises to Abraham and to Isaac and to Jacob. Notice the difference between Pharaoh and the Lord. Pharaoh doesn't remember who Joseph was, and he enslaves and oppresses the people. The Lord *does* remember Abraham, Isaac, and Jacob. And what does God do once God remembers God's promises? God calls Moses—the fugitive murderer.

The call story of Moses is one of the great scenes in the Old Testament. One day, Moses is out keeping watch over his father-in-law's sheep. [SPOILER ALERT: Whenever someone is shepherding a flock of sheep, God is going to call them to some important service, usually "shepherding" God's people.] Moses is doing what shepherds do— throwing rocks, picking up sticks, singing "Sweet Baby James"—when suddenly a bush bursts into flame, yet the bush itself isn't consumed! Then God speaks, "Take off your sandals! This is holy ground! I want you to go back to Egypt and lead my people out of slavery."

In most Old Testament call stories, the person God calls has an excuse for why they can't say yes to God's call, and keeping to the script, Moses offers a bunch of excuses! But God—in the form of the burning-but-not-consumed bush, gets up in Moses's face and confronts him with a holy calling.

God: "Moses, I'm the God of Abraham, Isaac, and Jacob. I've heard the cries of my people.

My heart is strangely warmed . . . [God goes on a while here about how much God's people are suffering] . . . So, come now, I will send you to Egypt and bring my people home."

Moses: "What me? Little ole' me? I'm just a nobody."

God: "No. Really. I am sending you and I will be with you and you will come out and worship me on this very mountain."

Moses: "Ummm. . . . Who would I say is sending me? I don't even know your name!"

God: "I am who I am! Tell them I AM has sent you. YHWH, God of Abraham, Isaac, and Jacob has sent you!"

Moses: "But what if they don't believe me? How will they know a talking/burning bush spoke to me?"

God: "That stick in your hand will turn to a snake and then turn back into a stick whenever you snap your fingers."

Moses: "O God! I don't even like public speaking! I stutter when I have to speak in front of crowds!"

God: "You think that I can't cure a stutter? I am God!"

Moses: "Please, please, please send someone else!"

God: "MOSES!!! Your brother Aaron will be with you; I will talk to you, and he will do the actual talking. I've already sent for him—he's on the way. And Moses—I've waited until now because the Pharaoh who was seeking to put you to death for that murder, he is dead. So go."

So Moses, with God up in his grill, overawed by God's intense holiness, agrees to go to Egypt and bring the people out of slavery.

Here is a fun fact. I once bowled on a bowling team called The Plagues. Pretty cool, huh? It wasn't a real team that bowled in a league or anything. It was just a charity thing where a bunch of Bible professors from the seminary where I work agreed to lose in bowling to some students. But we took our name from the throwdown that happens when Moses confronts Pharaoh with the demand, "Let my people go!" Pharaoh replies, "You need a hall pass to go to the restroom." Moses comes back at him, "Not that kind of 'go.' Let my people go from slavery—let them go home to their own land." "Oh," says Pharaoh, "No. And if you try to escape from slavery, I will kill each and every one of you."

A plague-themed bowling team could have some seriously intimidating shirts.

THE DEACON

The issue was simple. Whose people were the Israelites? Who was the lord of this enslaved people? Was Pharaoh Israel's lord? Did they belong to him and serve him?

Or was the Lord Israel's lord? Did Israel belong to the Lord. And the thing about pharaohs—or any other kind of dictator, for that matter—is that pharaohs tend to think that everything is theirs. And when challenged, well, pharaohs don't like being challenged.

Thus commences one of the most fateful confrontations in human history—the contest between God and Pharaoh for the lordship of God's blessed-to-be-a-blessing people. At stake is not just the fate of those human beings—although that is a pretty big deal to the men, women, and children who are enslaved by Pharaoh. At stake is God's faithfulness to God's promises. Because if Pharaoh wins, it means that God can't keep God's promises. Also at stake is God's mission to bless the world through Israel. Because God is on a mission to love, save, bless, and be reconciled to the entire world. And if Pharaoh wins, well, no divine mission.

The throwdown between God and Pharaoh consists of God saying, "Let my people go." Then Pharaoh says, "No." Then God sends a plague and follows up the plague by asking, "Ready to admit defeat and let my people go?" "Never!" Pharaoh responds. So God sends another plague. This question-plague-refusal cycle lasts ten rounds. God, who is the Creator, likes to work with creation to work the plague thing. The ten plagues are:

1. The Nile River is turned to blood
2. An infestation of frogs! (Because what is scarier than frogs?)
3. An infestation of lice
4. Swarms of flies (those nasty deer flies that bite so hard you bleed, I'm guessing)
5. Death of the Egyptian livestock

6. An epidemic of boils
7. Storm of hail (totally trashed the Egyptians' windshields)
8. An infestation of locusts
9. Darkness for three days
10. Death of every firstborn son in the land

The text has a curious detail. Repeatedly in the narrative it says both that "the Lord hardened Pharaoh's heart" but also that "Pharaoh hardened his heart" or sometimes simply "Pharaoh's heart was hardened." This is not a medical condition (although Pharaoh did eat a little too much bacon). This is a condition of the soul. It means that Pharaoh will not change his will—his desire to keep his slaves, his desire to slug it out with God. He has decided to fight this fight to the very end. But does God *make him* do this? Does he do it himself? Is it both?

Some say, "If God hardened Pharaoh's heart, it was unjust." Others say, "Hey, Pharaoh had it coming, so it wasn't unjust." Still others, "It was necessary to have all ten plagues to demonstrate God's full power." And others, "Pharaoh's choices formed his character, and then he couldn't change even when he wanted to." Perhaps this meme means that God gave Pharaoh the courage to keep fighting in order to make it a fair contest. I'm not convinced that any of the explanations are all that helpful. The plain meaning of the text seems to be that it is both God's desire and Pharaoh's desire to fight this confrontation out to the end. Maybe the good news is that God will not compromise with evil. Maybe. In the end, I have to admit that I'm not really sure what to make of this. It is a good thing that eternal life does not rest on solving theological problems!

THE DEACON

I am guessing that God didn't ask Jesus for advice here. I can't imagine Jesus saying, "Love all your enemies except their firstborn sons."

Before the last plague, the Lord gives Moses instructions for the first Passover. "Tonight I am going to send the angel of death to kill every firstborn male in the country. If the angel of death sees blood on a doorpost, the angel will pass over that house and not kill anyone in that home. Every household is to eat lamb tonight and they are to sprinkle some of the lamb's blood on the doorpost. Don't put any yeast in your bread because you won't have time to let it rise. Eat flatbread tonight. You are to eat with your traveling clothes on and your hiking boots laced up. At first light, when Pharaoh says you can go, make for the border as fast as you can." And that's exactly what happens. Jews keep the festival of the Passover every year to this day to remember that the Lord kept the Lord's promises.

But once the people are gone, Pharaoh misses his slaves. So he rolls out his chariots, he lines up his infantry, and he saddles up the cavalry. They go after Israel and catch up to them just as they reach the sea. For all appearances, it seems like Pharaoh has caught up to the people just before they got away. There is no escape. The sea behind them and Pharaoh's entire military might in front of them. Out of the frying pan and into the outhouse, as the saying goes.

I don't think I know that saying, but I can confirm a correlation between fried foods and time on the porcelain throne.

THE ELDER

You don't have to say everything you know, as the saying goes.

THE BISHOP

And God's people whine. "Was it because there weren't any graves in Egypt that you led us out here to die?" they ask Moses. "We were better off as slaves!" They have seen God's works, but they lose faith. Really!? This puts the whole idea of being a "people of little faith" in biblical context. They have seen God's works, but they lose faith.

What does God do in the face of such unbelief from God's people? God saves them, of course. God keeps God's promises. Moses raises his hands. The waters draw back. The people walk through the sea on dry land. When Pharaoh orders his armies forward in pursuit of the Israelites, the waters come crashing in.

Pharaoh, who has resisted God's creative purposes and has chosen to serve death and oppression rather than life and peace, dies at the hands of creation. (So to speak—creation doesn't really have hands.) On the other side, Moses and Miriam lead the singing:

> Sing to the Lord, for he has triumphed
>> gloriously;
>>> horse and rider he has thrown into the sea.
>>> (Exodus 15:1)

The Lord has won. The Israelites belong to God the Creator and not to any human dictator. The Lord has freed the slaves, kept the divine promises, and preserved God's blessed-to-be-a-blessing people for the mission of God.

In the Wilderness—From Complaint to Complaint (Exodus 16–18)

At every point of danger, God has been there for the people, preserving them from every threat from Pharaoh to the angel of death. In Exodus 16:1, it says that "the whole congregation of the Israelites departed from Elim." They go out into the wilderness. And in the wilderness . . .

. . . God's people whine some more. "If only we had died by the hand of the Lord in the land of Egypt, when we sat by the fleshpots and ate our fill of bread; for you have brought us out into this wilderness to kill this whole assembly with hunger" (16:3). By verse 3, the people have again already lost faith!

So God rains down bread from heaven on the people. Every day! Bread from heaven. It's white and flaky. When the people see it, they say, "WHAT?!" The way that a person asks "what?" in Hebrew is *"man?"* So Moses says,

I tend to see the journey through the wilderness as Israel's coming-of-age story, and an essential part of being a child is whining about travel.

THE BISHOP

"That's what we will call it. Manna." And every day God makes quail fall out of the sky so that they can have a little protein with their manna. So they walk a little farther into the wilderness. And in the wilderness . . .

. . . God's people whine. They can't find any water, so they accuse Moses, "Why did you bring us out of Egypt, to kill us and our children and livestock with thirst?" (Exodus 17:3). So Moses complains to God, "What am I supposed to do with this people? They're about to kill me!" So God shows Moses how to make water flow from a rock. And the people drink.

Throughout this part of the Bible, Israel is telling the truth about itself in a way that is really important. They call themselves a "stiff-necked people" and describe how again and again they either lose faith in God, sin against God, or quarrel with God and with Moses. At least part of the point here is that the Bible is telling us: God didn't pick the best of the best. God worked with what God had at hand. A quarrelsome, stiff-necked, whining people of little faith. Israel was not full of itself. Israel was exceedingly humble.

God's Mission People, Covenant People, and Free People (Exodus 19–20)

Speaking of God's mission, God finally gets the people where God wants them—to freedom. Moses brings the people to Mount Sinai (also called Mount Horeb)—back to where God had appeared to Moses in the burning-but-not-consumed shrubbery. And there, God enters into a solemn and holy covenant with the people. But first, God explains to the people that this was all about God's mission to love, save, and bless the world through the chosen, priestly people. And God says:

> I flew you out of Egypt on the wings of eagles. And I brought you to be mine! My people. So if you will obey me and be part of this covenant, you will be my one-and-only treasured people. The whole earth is mine, but you shall be for me *a kingdom of priests and a holy nation*! (Exodus 19:5–6)

Now, for those keeping score at home, this is the third divine-human covenant in the Bible. Each one includes at least two parties, each includes a promise, and each includes a sign. In the first, God made a covenant through Noah with all flesh, promising not to destroy all flesh—the sign was the rainbow. In the second, God made a covenant with Abraham and Sarah, promising land, descendants, a great name, and a blessed-to-be-a-blessing blessing—the sign was male circumcision. Here, in the third covenant, God makes a covenant with Moses and all Israel; they will be God's treasured people, they will keep God's law, and they will be God's priestly people—the sign of the covenant is the Sabbath.

I know enough about my minister I can't imagine choosing to be one. Couldn't being born into a priestly people easily feel overbearing?

THE ACOLYTE

So notice that in the Abrahamic and Mosaic covenants, there is a mission for the people to participate in. They are a people through whom God is working to bless all the families of the earth. They are to be a priestly people—a kingdom of priests and a holy nation—and of course priests are those who bless other people.

One thing to notice in all of this is that God freed the people from impossible bondage, from slavery and oppression in Egypt. "I brought you out." "I brought you to be mine." "I flew you out of Egypt on the wings of eagles." God's commitment to the people, as we are about to see, is that they will never have to have another human king to oppress them. God promises to be their lord directly. To be a free people, a treasured people from all the people of the earth. What a gift! Freedom.

And what is freedom? Freedom is relationship with God. Notice that God says, "I brought you to be mine!" This phrase can be—and usually is—translated as, "I brought you to me." And that is legitimate. But the point is the relationship between God and people. God didn't bring them "to me" in the sense of a location—God brought the people "to me" in the sense of a relationship. Freedom with God is all about relationship.

THE ELDER

In a world without source or purpose, freedom pertains to one's own ability to choose, but as a part of God's creation, true freedom is the freedom to know and love God. This makes me uncomfortable.

The Covenant Law—The Ten Commandments (Exodus 20)

CHAPTER 4, OPTIONAL QUEST #2: READ EXODUS 19–23 (COMPLETE QUEST AND LEVEL UP TO DELIVERANCE STAR, LEVEL 2).

Then God does an amazing, miraculous thing. God shows this recently freed, formerly enslaved people *how free people live!* People need training in freedom. Freedom is a very hard thing to master. Just leave your teenage child— or sibling, or self—home alone for a week. When you come back a day early, what are you going to find? All the laundry done? The house neat? The yard mowed? The dishes done? Maybe. Maybe not.

To learn to live free, you need guidelines. And you need practice. So God gives the people guidelines. And, according to God, here is how free people live:

I am the Lord your God, who brought you out of the land of Egypt, out of the house of slavery!

1. You shall never have any other God but me—you never have to serve another human king, like Pharaoh.
2. Never worship any idol or any carved statue—neither a statue of me, or of some other false god, or of any angel or demon.
3. Never misuse my name—don't say "I swear to God" and then tell a lie; don't pretend you are a good person of faith and then do something crappy to your neighbor.
4. One day out of seven—we'll call it the Sabbath—everyone gets a day off; not just the property owners or parents, but everyone, including children, the poor, and the animals.
5. Honor your parents—when they get old, sick, or disabled, you must take care of them.
6. Never murder.
7. Never have sex with someone you're not married to.
8. Never steal—either illegal stealing or legal stealing.
9. Never use your words to hurt either your friend or your enemy—never say, "I hate to say it" and then say it; never say, "bless her heart" and then say something horrible about a person—even if it's true!
10. Never covet anything that is your neighbor's—to covet means to "want it so bad that you start to scheme to get from your neighbor." Because once you set your heart on scheming to get something from your neighbor, well, bad crap happens—usually to both you and your neighbor.

THE DEACON

> I'm not down with making big statues of the big ten, but if we had to, this version might be more instructive for our legal system.

And that, my friends, is how free people live. These laws are known as the Ten Commandments. Or *Ten Words*.

The purpose of God's law is life—the very existence of creation and the existence within creation of life. God's law is about creating a safe and trustworthy space in which life can exist and in which life can be good. God's law—as expressed in the Ten Commandments—is about creating the conditions for the good life. Through the law, God is all about creating the conditions for a more trustworthy society and life.

But as a friend of mine who is very good at math likes to say, "nineteen comes before twenty." That is, Exodus 19 comes before Exodus 20. And I would add that Exodus 20:1 comes before Exodus 20:2–17.

In Exodus 19, God says, "I flew you out of Egypt on the wings of eagles. I brought you out to be mine. I am making you my own treasured people." Then, Exodus 20, God gives the law—"Do this. Don't do that. Can't you read the two stone tablets?"

Even in Exodus 20, God first says, "I am the Lord your God who brought you out of the land of Egypt, out of the house of slavery." And only then does God say, "Do this. Don't do that. Can't you read the two stone tablets?"

What's the point? The relationship comes before the law. God frees the people and establishes the relationship. Only then does God give the law. In other words, God doesn't say, "In order to earn the right to be my people, you must first keep these rules." Rather, God says, "You are my people. I have freed you. Now here are some laws about how free people live."

The law is not a means to relationship with God. God establishes the relationship and then gives the law as the way that people in a relationship of freedom live.

The primary purpose of the law is love. What God is doing through the law is teaching us how to love our neighbors. Imagine this conversation between God and you.

God: "I am going to teach you my will and plan for your life."

You: "Sweet. I cannot wait to know your will and plan. Have you decided who I will marry?"

God: "Technically, with proper grammar, that should be, 'whom I will marry.' But no, I don't have that kind of plan for your life. That isn't how I work. I will give you guidance in life, but you will decide whom you marry. And your spouse will get a choice in the matter, obviously."

You: "What sort of plan do you have for my life, then, if you aren't going to make all of my decisions for me?"

God: "Here is my plan. Love me. Love your neighbor. I spoke these words in the Bible. 'You shall love the Lord your God with all your heart, and all your soul, and all your might' (Deuteronomy 6:5). 'Love your neighbor as yourself' (Leviticus 19:18). In summary: Love me and love your neighbor. Any questions."

You: "Yes. One question. How do I love my neighbor?"

God: "How do you love your neighbor? Don't kill, commit adultery, or steal from your neighbor. Take care of the elderly. Everyone gets a day off. Don't use your words to hurt your neighbor. Don't scheme to get your neighbor's stuff."

You see, the law is a guide to how to love the neighbor. It is all about love.

THE DEACON

The idea that God has a plan for your life can be pretty terrifying regularly tell my students, "God doesn't have a plan for your life, but a purpose for your living."

Second, the law requires interpretation. The heart of the law—the Ten Commandments—never changes. It is God's eternal will that we not murder, steal, commit adultery, use our words to hurt our neighbor, abandon the elderly, and so on.

But as times and situations change, our interpretation of and application of the law must change, too.

Imagine this conversation. Between God and, let's say, Moses, representing all of Israel.

God: "Here is a great law. Do not steal. Can you manage that?"

Moses: "Absolutely. I won't steal. But can I break into my neighbor's farm and take my neighbor's ox or donkey?"

[Note: In the ancient agricultural world, your ox and donkey were probably your most valuable possessions—sort of like your tractor and your pickup truck today. So a lot of the laws are about oxen and donkeys.]

God: "No! You cannot take your neighbor's ox or donkey. That is what 'do not steal' means."

Moses: "What if my ox gets in a fight with my neighbor's ox and kills it? Is that the same as stealing my neighbor's ox?"

God: "Sometimes the answer is 'yes' and sometimes it is 'no.' I spoke regarding this matter in Exodus 21:35–36, 'If someone's ox kills the ox of another, then they shall sell the live ox and divide the price of it; and the dead animal they shall also divide. But if it was known that the ox was accustomed to gore in the past, and its owner has not restrained it, the owner shall restore ox for ox, but keep the dead animal.'"

Moses: "What if my neighbor's ox falls in a pit I was digging and dies? Is that the same as stealing?"

God: "Sometimes yes and sometimes no. I have spoken in Exodus 21:33–34, 'If someone leaves a pit open, or digs a pit and does not cover it, and an ox or a donkey falls into it, the owner of the pit shall make restitution, giving money to its owner, but keeping the dead animal.' But note that if you didn't put up orange crime-scene tape marking the pit, and a fence to keep ox and donkeys out, then you are guilty."

Moses: "God, if my neighbor's ox or donkey wanders away from her farm and I see it and if I don't help because it is raining and I am watching football and don't want to go out in the cold, and then the ox or donkey dies, is that stealing?"

God: "Not only your neighbor's ox, but your enemy's ox—you *must* help. I have spoken in Exodus 23:4–5: 'When you come upon your enemy's ox or donkey going astray, you shall bring it back. When you see the donkey of one who hates you lying under its burden and you would hold back from setting it free, you must help to set it free.'"

You get the point. Deciding what *stealing* is and what we must all do to keep the law against stealing is very complicated. It requires constant interpretation and constant application to changing society.

Just imagine a world in which we can steal another person's identity! Imagine a world in which we can "bear false witness against our neighbor" on social media like Facebook, Snapchat, and the like. Imagine how we can break the commandment against stealing when we sell information about our neighbors on the internet?

Moses's line of
questioning reminds
me of my very litigious
firstborn. She always

THE BISHOP

wanted to follow the rules but hoped there
was enough grey to get even with her
brother.

A Long Journey of Law and Growing in Freedom (Exodus 24–Joshua 1)

> CHAPTER 4, OPTIONAL QUEST #3: READ
> EXODUS 32, DEUTERONOMY 5 AND 26
> (COMPLETE QUEST AND LEVEL UP TO
> DELIVERANCE STAR, LEVEL 3).

Essentially, the rest of Exodus, Leviticus, Numbers, and Deuteronomy is an extended travel story in which Israel journeys through the wilderness. There are various stories of sin, interrupted by God forgiving and then giving new laws and offering new blessings, moments of guidance, and experiences of grace.

Think about these chapters and books of the Bible as sort of like Israel's high-school years. Or maybe teenage years.

Assuming you have passed through your teen years already, what do you remember about your teenage years? You probably remember things like this:

- Really great moments of achievement or significant milestones. Like graduating from high school or getting your first job. Or like when Israel and God made a covenant at Mount Sinai and God gave Israel the job of being a nation of priests.

- Really awful moments of failure and brokenness. Like your first car crash, or your first moment of really screwing up something major; your parents got really mad, but I hope they forgave you. Or like when Israel made a golden calf to worship because they didn't know what had happened to Moses—see Exodus 32. God got really mad, but Moses walked God back from the edge, and God forgave the people.

- Really awesome lessons from important teachers and coaches. Like the great class you had from Herr Rockey, your high-school German teacher. Or that life changing class from Mr. Fox about College Prep English. Or that fantastic tennis coach who changed your life. Or maybe that really important lesson Israel learned about how to love the neighbor. Or the key lesson Israel learned about trusting God, even when it looked like trusting God was really foolhardy.

- Really awesome moments of experiencing God's guidance. Like when you weren't sure what to do after high school, but you felt God's presence lead you to make a good decision—about what trade to learn, or to join the armed services, or which college to attend, or what to do with a year of service. Or like when God led Israel through the wilderness as a pillar of cloud by day and a pillar of fire by night. And God provided manna and quail for the people to eat every single day.

- Really great first relationships with a special some-one. Like. Hmmm. I better not mention her name here. It didn't last, but it was awesome for a while. When Israel looked back at these wilderness years later, Israel remembered them as good years, with God teaching and leading the people and the peo-ple learning how it is that free people life. At times, God was like that tennis coach who really got in your face and made you better—even though you almost quit three times, and of course there was that day with the donuts on court 12. At times God was like that band director who made you play the horn part that you hadn't practiced; he made you play it three times, and you failed all three times. By the end, the whole band knew that you hadn't practiced, and you were wasting everyone's time. It was humiliating. But you learned.

The funny thing about this long and winding road that Israel took through the wilderness is that it is filled with odd stories of failure, of sin, of rebellion, of lack of trust. Read it and see.

The books are also filled with all sorts of laws and instructions. Here are some of the most important laws, selectively chosen for your enjoyment and for your edification.

How to Bless Someone

The Lord spoke to Moses, saying: Speak to Aaron and his descendants, saying, "Thus you shall bless the Israelites: You shall say to them"

The Lord bless you and keep you;

the Lord make his face to shine upon you, and be gracious to you;

the Lord lift up his countenance upon you, and give you peace.

So they shall put my name on the Israelites, and I will bless them. (Numbers 6:22–27)

How to Treat the Marginalized and Disabled

You shall not defraud your neighbor; you shall not steal; and you shall not keep for yourself the wages of a laborer until morning. You shall not revile the deaf or put a stumbling block before the blind; you shall fear your God: I am the Lord. (Leviticus 19:13–14)

How Not to Treat Women

Do not profane your daughter by making her a prostitute, that the land not become prostituted and full of depravity. You shall keep my sabbaths and reverence my sanctuary: I am the Lord. (Leviticus 19:29–30)

The Most Important Thing Moses Ever Said (The Great Shema)

Hear, O Israel: The Lord is our God, the Lord is One. You shall love the Lord your God with all your heart, and with all your soul, and with all your might. Keep these words that I am commanding you today in your heart. Recite them to your children and talk about them when you are at home and when you are away, when you lie down and when you rise. Bind them as a sign on your hand, fix them as an emblem on your forehead, and write them on the doorposts of your house and on your gates. (Deuteronomy 6:4–9)

How to Tell a False Prophet from a True Prophet

"Any prophet who speaks in the name of other gods, or who is presumptuous enough to speak in my name a word that I have not commanded the prophet to speak—that prophet shall die." You might say to yourself, "How can we recognize a word that the Lord has not spoken?" If a prophet speaks in the name of the Lord but the thing does not take place or prove true, it is a word that the Lord has not spoken. The prophet has spoken it presumptuously; do not be frightened by it. (Deuteronomy 18:20–22)

What "Tithes" Are Really For

Set apart a tithe of all the yield of your seed that is brought in yearly from the field. In the presence of the Lord your God, in the place that he will choose as a dwelling for his name, you shall eat the tithe of your grain, your wine, and your oil, as well as the firstlings of your herd and flock, so that you may learn to fear the Lord your God always . . . go to the place that the Lord your God will choose;

spend the money for whatever you wish—oxen, sheep, wine, strong drink, or whatever you desire. And you shall eat there in the presence of the Lord your God, you and your household rejoicing together. As for the Levites resident in your towns, do not neglect them . . . as well as the resident aliens, the orphans, and the widows in your towns, may come and eat their fill so that the Lord your God may bless you in all the work that you undertake. (Deuteronomy 14:22–29)

How to Keep God from Stepping in It

You shall have a designated area outside the camp to which you shall go. With your utensils you shall have a trowel; when you relieve yourself outside, you shall dig a hole with it and then cover up your excrement. Because the Lord your God travels along with your camp, to save you and to hand over your enemies to you, therefore your camp must be holy, so that he may not see anything indecent among you and turn away from you. (Deuteronomy 23:12–14)

And so on. The many and various laws of the Pentateuch are totally fun. Except when they're totally weird or icky. But mostly fun. There are laws about not eating road kill. There are laws about not plowing your field with an ox and donkey yoked together. There are laws about which kinds of insects you can eat and which you cannot eat. I don't know about you, but I don't eat any insects—other than an occasional bug I swallow when I am out riding my bicycle too fast and I inhale one. Yuck.

Moses's Long Goodbye (Deuteronomy)

Moses is probably the most important human in the Old Testament. Unless it is David. Unless it is Abraham and Sarah. Unless it is Isaiah. Anyway, I'm going with Moses.

Moses is the *deliverer* par excellence in the Old Testament, the *covenant maker* par excellence, the *law giver* par excellence, and also the *leader* par excellence. God does all the miracle working, of course. But working in the power of God, Moses delivers the people from Egypt, Moses leads the people to enter into the covenant that God established at Sinai, Moses downloads God's law and helps the people imagine how to apply it to life, and Moses leads the people through forty years of wandering from Egypt to Sinai to the edge of the promised land.

And then, standing on a mountain just to the east of the Jordan River, Moses looks over into the promised land and has one last talk with God.

> Moses: "God, tomorrow we go into the promised land. You are about to put the final icing on this big old cake of promise keeping. You promised that we would become a great nation. And we are. You promised that we would be blessed and through us you would bless the rest of the families of the earth. You've done that. You have promised us a great name. And we have that now—every nation knows the name of Israel. And now, you keep the promise of the land. Tomorrow I will lead the people across the river and back into our home."
>
> God: "Moses, I've got some good news and some bad news. The good news is that indeed, I

am keeping my promise. Tomorrow the people cross over the river and will be home."

Moses: "Hit me with the bad news, God."

God: "Moses, you aren't going. You've led the people well these forty years and more. But you don't get to go into the land. Take a good look now across the river. And say goodbye. Joshua will lead the people into the land."

Moses: "God! That is not fair!"

God: "Moses, the fair is in August. It is where they judge the sheep and the goats. But I have a nice consolation prize for you. You get to give a long goodbye speech. One day, they will call that speech the book of Deuteronomy."

THE BISHOP

I served one extremely difficult congregation over the years, and oh how I wish that God had granted me the opportunity to give them a long goodbye speech.

So Moses, the man of God, gives his long goodbye speech. He led the people out of Egypt—teaching them that the God of Israel is a deliverer, who bought the people out of slavery. He led the people to God and God's covenant—teaching the people that God is a God of covenant promises, always keeping God's promises. He led the people through the wilderness—teaching the people to follow

God's guidance, trusting in God's purposes for them and for the world. He taught the people God's law—teaching the people that God is law, that God's law is about love for the neighbor and for God.

And then Moses has one more lesson. That God will always raise up leaders for the next generation of faithful people. And so Moses passes the torch to Joshua.

Moses gives his long goodbye speech. Then Moses blesses each of the tribes of Israel. And then he dies.

Where they buried Moses, they would not say. Nobody knows. "Never since has there arisen a prophet in Israel like Moses, whom the Lord knew face to face. He was unequaled for all the signs and wonders that the Lord sent him to perform in the land of Egypt, against Pharaoh and all his servants and his entire land, and for all the mighty deeds and all the terrifying displays of power that Moses performed in the sight of all Israel" (Deuteronomy 34:10–12).

Into the Land (Joshua)

The book of Joshua tells the story of how Israel entered the promised land. It is a tough story. For me, as an Old Testament scholar, this is the worst part of the Old Testament. According to the story, Israel crosses over, and Joshua leads a violent conquest of the promised land, taking the land back from the Canaanites, who are living there prior to the rearrival of Abraham and Sarah's descendants.

CHAPTER 4, OPTIONAL QUEST #4: READ JOSHUA 1–9, 24 (COMPLETE QUEST AND LEVEL UP TO DELIVERANCE STAR, LEVEL 4).

THE ELDER

Can I skip Deliverance Star, Level 4 and avoid Joshua's killing spree? It is pretty embarrassing.

The message of the book of Joshua is to be "strong and courageous" in the Lord. Here is the key opening exhortation to Joshua: "Be strong and courageous" (Joshua 1:6). Strength and courage in the Lord here require three things. First, taking possession of the land. Second, being devoted to God's word. Third, being confident in God and not being afraid to follow God's lead.

But there is a dark side here. In order to possess the land, people die. And the book of Joshua says that God commanded it to be so. There is the comforting-yet-harrowing tale of Rahab, the prostitute who sells out her people in order to join with the invading Israelites. And the delightful story of marching around the walls of Jericho blowing trumpets and playing "Seventy-Six Trombones" until the very walls themselves cannot stand the sound and simply collapse rather than hear another note.

The worst part of the worst part starts in chapter 8, where God commands the people to utterly destroy the Canaanites—especially the inhabitants of Ai. "Israel had finished slaughtering all the inhabitants of Ai in the open wilderness . . . according to the word of the Lord that he had issued to Joshua" (Joshua 8:24–27). Did God really command this? If so, why? How does this square with a God who swore off violence after the great flood? If not, why did Israel say God did? Did it really happen? Probably not, but how does that help? Very troubling.

Fortunately, the conquest of the land is not the end of the story—either of God keeping promises or, perhaps, of God learning that violence doesn't work with a broken creation.

You Cannot Serve the Lord—Really, You Can't (The History of Israel and Judah; Joshua 23–2 Kings)

O nce they settle the land, each tribe has their own geographical territory—except for the nonterritorial, priestly tribe of Levi. The Levites are spread throughout the land, with priests living and serving in all towns and cities. The Levites are given towns throughout the land within the territory of the other tribes, but they are not given territory.

No Money for Maps: Wouldn't it be cool to have a nice map here that shows the boundaries of where the twelve tribes settled in the land? But there's no money for maps! So just Google it or open up a good Bible—they all have nice maps.

According to the book of Joshua, for the rest of the life of Joshua, son of Nun, the Israelites had "rest from their enemies." Here, *rest* means not a nice nap but peace and security from war. Joshua grew old and the time of his death drew near.

The Covenant Renewed and the Plot of Joshua 24–2 Kings: You Cannot Serve the Lord

CHAPTER 5, OPTIONAL QUEST #1: READ JOSHUA 24 (COMPLETE QUEST AND LEVEL UP TO OT HISTORIAN, FRESHMAN LEVEL).

This block of Israel's history stretches all the way through the end of the book of 2 Kings—if you're interested in details, check out this fancy endnote.[1] Let's call this block of narrative the "history of Israel and Judah." One of the common features of this history is that from time to time, key figures in Israel and Judah's history give extended farewell speeches at the end of their lives. Joshua is one of those figures.

In Joshua 24, near the end of his life, Joshua gathers the leaders of the tribes of Israel together to give his farewell speech, leads the tribes in renewing the covenant between Israel and God, and then establishes the plot for the history of Israel and Judah.

Joshua's speech begins by summarizing God's gracious and saving acts on Israel's behalf: the call of Abraham, Isaac, and Jacob; the deliverance of Israel from Egypt via Moses and Aaron; the guidance of Israel through the wilderness years; and the leading of the people into the promised land. Then, Joshua exhorts the people to be faithful to the Lord:

And now, fear the Lord! Serve him wholly and faithfully. . . . But if it seems wrong in your eyes to serve the Lord, choose this day whom you will serve, either the gods your ancestors served beyond the river or the gods of the Amorites in whose land you are now dwelling. But as for me and my house, we will serve the Lord. (Joshua 24:14–15)

Joshua's statement of faith—"as for me and my house, we will serve the Lord"—is one of the most famous lines from the Old Testament. The people answer, "Because the Lord is our God—he who brought us out of the land of Egypt out of the house of slavery—and who did these great things in our sight . . . we will also serve the Lord" (24:17–18).

My neighbor is a fundamentalist preacher, and he is convinced this passage is related to prayer in public schools and the display of Thomas Kinkade paintings.

THE ELDER

But then Joshua says a strange thing. Having just asked the people to serve the Lord and having just promised to serve the Lord himself and having just gotten the answer that he clearly wanted, he counters, "You cannot serve the Lord, for he is a holy God!" (24:19). But the people insist, "We will serve the Lord!" "Very well," says Joshua. "Now therefore put away all your other gods and serve the Lord." Then the text says, "So Joshua made a covenant with the people that day" (24:25).

Several crucial ideas are at work here. The first is the idea of "renewing the covenant." The point is both that God's covenantal promises from the past endure into future generations, but they need to be renewed each generation. God's people must renew their faith and commitment to God in each generation. The second weighty idea here is that, simply put, "you cannot serve the Lord, for he is a holy God." We are back to one of the first concepts with which we started—God's holiness. What is God's holiness? It is the very presence of God. A presence too intense to endure. It is a sound too loud to bear. God's holiness demands that God's people be holy like God—putting away all objects of love other than two—God and the neighbors God has given us to love.

Christian theology has a fancy Latin phrase that clarifies this concept. That phrase is *non posse non peccare*, which means "it is not possible not to sin." No human being—born into a broken world as all of us are—can perfectly love God or neighbor. Nor can we perfectly set aside all of the objects of love—we call them *idols* or *false gods* in the theological business. This is the truth about each one of us as individuals. And it is the truth about all of us as communities.

The Plot

The phrase "you cannot serve the Lord" and the people's response "we will serve the Lord" thus set up the plot for the rest of the books of Israel's history up to the Babylonian exile—Judges, 1–2 Samuel, and 1–2 Kings.

The question is: Can Israel serve the Lord? Is Joshua right? Or are the people right? Let's keep going, because I for one cannot wait to find out.

Can the People Serve God When Led by Tribes and Judges (Book of Judges)

> CHAPTER 5, OPTIONAL QUEST #2: READ JUDGES (COMPLETE QUEST AND LEVEL UP TO OT HISTORIAN, SOPHOMORE LEVEL).

Then Joshua, son of Nun, dies. After Joshua dies, he is not succeeded by a single leader. Rather than being led by one individual, each tribe has their own leadership. But from time to time—when a crisis dictates it or need calls for it—this happens: "The Lord raised up judges and they delivered them from the hand of their oppressors" (Judges 2:16).

The time period of the judges covers roughly 1240 BCE until 1000 BCE.

A *judge* was not a judge like we think of them—in ancient Israel, a judge was a charismatic leader who would lead Israel against its enemies. If that leader was successful in battle and victorious over Israel's enemies, then people within Israel would go to that person to have him or her (judges could be female) judge their legal disputes—hence the name.

According to Judges, it becomes apparent rather quickly that, when organized by the tribe and led by charismatic judges, Israel indeed *cannot* serve the Lord. A rather predictable pattern of behavior results:

1. Israel fails to serve the Lord, instead worshiping false gods.
2. God allows Israel to be dominated by a neighboring country.
3. As when they were in Egypt, the people "cried out to the Lord."
4. God raises up a deliverer who will deliver them from their oppressor.
5. For the remainder of the deliverer's life, he or she judges Israel and Israel has "rest."
6. Rinse and repeat as many times as necessary until you realize that as long as you are organized by the tribe and led by judges, you cannot serve the Lord (see Judges 2:16–23).

The book of Judges contains more than just stories about judges. In between the stories about judges are stories of incredible sin and brokenness. Because of the stories about judges and because of some preexisting notions that the Bible must be a *book of virtue*, some people have assumed that Judges is a book of Israel's heroes. That's not the case. Judges is a book that describes the human condition as the condition of being broken—unable to love God or neighbor perfectly, not able not to sin, and prone to wandering off after other gods. Here are some of Israel's most important judges and some of the most important stories of sin and brokenness.

Othniel—Othniel's story is only told in brief, but he delivers Israel from the Syrians. His gift appears to be strength in battle. (Judges 3)

Ehud—One of the most funny and gross stories in the Bible, the story of Ehud the judge and Eglon, the king of

Moab, is a favorite story for many junior-high boys—and not a few girls. Ehud's gift is guile. King Eglon, who is morbidly obese, imposes a harsh annual tax on Israel. Ehud volunteers to deliver the tax. As Eglon is sitting on the toilet—apparently he is constipated—Ehud slips into the privy, slips out a concealed sword (don't worry, God issued him a conceal-and-carry permit), and then slips it straight into the fattest part of Eglon's belly. Constipation relieved. (Judges 3)

When my youth minister growing up discovered a clogged and stinky toilet during a lock-in, he asked, "who pulled an Eglon in the bathroom?"

THE DEACON

Deborah—Deborah, who is also a prophet, delivers Israel from King Jabin of Canaan. Deborah's gift is leadership. She unites most of the tribes of Israel to face Jabin in battle, where Jabin's general Sisera is defeated. Sisera flees, but a woman named Jael pounds a tent peg through his brain while he sleeps. Jael nails it. Then Deborah, like the prophet Miriam before her, sings a song of victory—that song of victory in Judges 5 is one of the oldest poems in the Old Testament. (Judges 4–5)

Gideon—Gideon delivers the Israelites from the Midianites. He is a dog lover, apparently, whose gift is faith—until it isn't. Gideon gathers a great army to battle the Midianites, but God wants Gideon to win not with numbers but with faith. First, God sends home anyone who is afraid. Then, watching the troops drink from a river, God sends home anyone who cups water in his hands in order to drink. The three hundred who are left all stuck their faces in the water and lapped it up like dogs. With these three hundred, ill-mannered, water-slurping "dawgs"—who are a little less impressive than the three hundred Spartans King Leonidas led to battle at Thermopylae—Gideon wins. After the Israelites try to make him king, "I will not rule over you, my son will not rule over you, only the Lord will rule over you," he responds (Judges 8:23). Nicely done! Faith in action! "Oh, but how about you each give me a gold earring!" With these earrings, he makes a golden ephod, before which Israel worships. We don't know what an ephod was, but Israel was supposed to make no graven images. Ill done. Un-faith in action. (Judges 6–8)

"Milly" the Tower Woman—Abimelech is sort of an anti-judge. Unlike Gideon, he wants to be king. He raises a force and kills seventy of his closest friends and relatives and then rules for three years. In the course of trying to put down a rebellion, Abimelech attacks a strong tower at Thebez. A certain woman throws a heavy millstone from the tower at his head—I like to call her Milly. And Milly crushes it. (Judges 9)

Jephthah and His Daughter—One of the saddest stories is that of Jephthah and his daughter. Jephthah's gift is that he is a great warrior, but he is rash. He defeats the Ammonites in battle and swears a rash vow, forgetting that God has commanded Israel not to make vows in the name of the Lord. He vows to the Lord, "If you help us win I will offer in sacrifice the first living thing that I see" (Judges 11:31). You guessed it. Jephthah wins and then he sees his daughter—his only daughter, his only child. She asks for and is granted two months to dance and rejoice with her friends. "So there arose an Israelite custom that for four days every year the daughters of Israel would go out to lament the daughter of Jephthah" (11:40). (By the way, there is no hint that God actually expected Jephthah to keep that rash vow. Maybe his superstition led him to keep it.) (Judges 11)

Samson and Delilah—The story of Samson and his Philistine wife Delilah is well known. Even the Grateful Dead have a song about them. Samson is not a hero—his gift is strength. He marries poorly—and so does Delilah his wife. He defeats the Philistines in battle, so Delilah betrays him. In captivity, chained to pillar in a Philistine temple in order to be mocked, he manages to pull down the pillar and the building. Many die. The chorus to the Grateful Dead's song goes: "If I had my way, if I had my way, if I had my way, I would tear this old building down." (Judges 13–16)

Toward the end of Judges, we get two devastating, editorial comments from whomever wrote this book:

- "In those days there was no king in Israel." (18:1)
- "In those days, when there was no king in Israel . . ." (19:1)

The Priest's Wife—After those two comments follows what I take to be the ugliest story in the Old Testament—the horrible, tragic story of the Levite's concubine. A Levite was a priest, and a concubine was a wife. So this is a story about a priest and his wife. While traveling from her father's home in Bethlehem back to his home in Ephraim, nobody in the region of Gibeah will offer the priest and his wife hospitality. God's law says that people should welcome and offer hospitality to strangers. Finally, an old man takes them in. Some criminals from Gibeah come to the home and demand that the priest be sent out so that they can rape him. The priest, noble and obedient only to himself, instead pushes his wife outside. They rape her until she dies. (Judges 19)

The book of Judges ends: "In those days there was no king in Israel; all the people did what was right in their own eyes" (21:25). Or, apparently, what was wrong in their own eyes.

THE ACOLYTE

It has to be pretty bad for women to think having a king would help.

As already noted, one message of Judges is that the human condition is a truly broken reality. We suck. We are sinful. We are born into a broken world—where people try to rule over us. And when there are deliverers or saviors, we think that they might be different—but they, too, are imperfect. And even the best of them are still sinners. We are people who need to be free from the oppressive power of others—but when we are free, we cannot handle that freedom.

An important feature to note in Judges relates to the health of women. At the start of the book, Israel is led by Deborah—who is a judge, a leader, a prophetess, and a singer. The defeat of Sisera requires the strength of Jael and the defeat of Abimelech requires the strength of Milly. Jael nails it and Milly crushes it. As the book progresses, we find Jephthah's daughter unjustly sacrificed to God. Then Delilah betrays Samson. And at the end the horrible treatment of the priest's wife—both by her so-called husband and by her murderers. A message here is that in a god-fearing, righteous society, women do well. Where women are more free, closer to equal, and relatively safe—you can see the hand of God. Where women are less free, more unequal, and relatively endangered— you can see the hand of men.

And a final message of Judges is that we cannot serve the Lord as free or as loosely organized groups. Cannot do it. Israel could not serve the Lord perfectly. And neither can we. "In those days there was no king in Israel; all the people did what was right in their own eyes" (Judges 21:25).

Ruth (Book of Ruth)

CHAPTER 5, OPTIONAL QUEST #3: READ RUTH (COMPLETE QUEST AND LEVEL UP TO OT HISTORIAN, JUNIOR LEVEL).

The book of Ruth is set in the time of the Judges, but none of the characters in the book are judges. This book— nestled neatly between Judges and 1 Samuel—is a brief interlude in Israel's story, and it reminds us that even in the worst of times, people can be beautiful, faithful, and generous. Even in the darkest of nights, the light of love can shine through.

Naomi lives in Bethlehem with her husband and two sons, but they have to flee to Moab because of a famine. While in Moab, her sons marry—to Ruth and to Orpah—but then all three men die. Naomi tells her daughters-in-law that she will head back to Bethlehem but urges them to return to their fathers' houses. Orpah returns home, but Ruth remains loyal to Naomi, speaking beautiful words of human love:

> Where you go, I will go;
> > Where you sleep, I will sleep.
> Your people are my people,
> > Your God is my God.
> Where you die, I will die;
> > there I will be buried. (Ruth 1:16–17)

Life on the road is dangerous for two women. When they return home at harvest, they go to "glean" in the fields—meaning to pick up whatever stray grain the harvesters dropped. A distant relative of Naomi—Boaz by name—looks out for Ruth. He makes sure she is safe and that she gets plenty of barley. And Ruth looks out for him—a lonely single guy—offering herself in love and marriage. In the story, Ruth and Boaz save each other from meaninglessness. Ruth and Naomi also save each other from the danger of a world of men. And then Ruth bears Boaz a son—who is Naomi's grandson. The women of the village lay the baby on Naomi's bosom and say these beautiful words: "He shall restore your thirst for life and bring fulfillment to you in old age. *For your daughter-in-law who loves you, who is more to you than seven sons*, has given birth to him" (Ruth 4:15). Who is more to you than seven sons! Who loves you! What joy!

Naomi's grandson's name is Obed. Obed's grandson is David. *That* David.

Israel Demands a King Other than God (1 Samuel)

CHAPTER 5, OPTIONAL QUEST #4: READ 1 SAMUEL 1–9 (COMPLETE QUEST AND LEVEL UP TO OT HISTORIAN, SENIOR LEVEL).

The question for debate before the house is: "Can Israel serve the Lord?" Organized as individuals, loosely grouped, and led by judges, the answer is: No. Israel cannot serve the Lord.

Can Israel serve the Lord if led and organized in other ways? That is the question that the books of 1–2 Samuel and 1–2 Kings take up. But first, how does Israel get to the point of having kings? That transition is described in 1 Samuel 1–9.

As is so often the case in the Bible, the story of God's faithfulness to God's promises and to God's people picks up in what seems to be the most unlikely of circumstances—just when things don't seem like they can get any worse. And we're back to the story of a woman—Hannah. The period of the judges seems to end with the condition of women in Israel being fraught with danger and injustice. But then there's the book of Ruth—in which both Naomi and Ruth thrive in the end—followed by the story of Hannah.

Like so many women in the Bible, Hannah is childless. To make matters worse, as was common in those days, Hannah's husband has another wife—Peninnah. Peninnah has children. Hannah has none. Peninnah needles Hannah and makes her life miserable. But Hannah's husband loves her. And in the end, the Lord gives her children. Foreshadowing words that Mary the mother of Jesus would later sing, Hannah sings: "My heart exults in the Lord! My honor is lifted up in the Lord!" (1 Samuel 2:1)

Hannah gives birth to Samuel. When Samuel is old enough to go away to boarding school, she sends him to serve with Eli—the chief priest at Shiloh, which is where they keep the Ten Commandments in the ark of the covenant. Eli is faithful, but he is old. And Eli's sons—who according to ancient custom are to be priests and leaders after him—steal from the people's offering and have sex with the prostitutes who turn tricks at the entrance to the tent of meeting.

One night, as Samuel sleeps near the ark of the covenant, God calls, "Samuel! Samuel!" Samuel goes to Eli and says, "What is it, why did you call?" "Go back to sleep," says Eli, "It's just a dream." Three times God calls. Three times Samuel goes to Eli. Three times Eli says, "Go back to bed." But on the third time, he adds, "If it happens again, it is God. And say, 'Speak Lord, for your servant hears.'"

"Samuel! Samuel!" God calls. And Samuel answers, "Speak Lord, for your servant hears."

Samuel's first job is to fire Eli and his kids. In the morning, Eli asks, "Did God speak to you?" He sees that Samuel is afraid, so he says, "If it is bad news, I can take it." And it is. Because Eli let his sons steal from the people of God and have sex with the prostitutes who plague the holy place of God, God fires Eli. Eli says, "Let God do what is right in his eyes." In the years that follow, Samuel serves well as judge of Israel. He is a trustworthy prophet, and God speaks faithfully through him. And so, when Samuel grows old . . .

. . . Israel again whines. "Hey God! We are surrounded by nations and people who have kings. Eli was okay as a priest, but his sons were craptacular. Samuel has been alright as a prophet and a judge, but his sons take bribes when they judge legal matters. So give us a king! We want a king! We want a king! We want a king!"

And God says, "Samuel, they aren't rejecting you, they are rejecting me as their king. So I will do what they want and give them a king. But first, you have to go and tell them what kings are like."

Kings! What are they good for? Absolutely nothing.

THE ELDER

So Samuel speaks to Israel and says, "You say you want a king. Here is what kings are good for. A king will take your sons and force them to be soldiers in his armies and workers for his massive building projects—like building himself a huge palace. He will take your daughters to serve as his sex toys, his cooks, and his cleaners. He will tax you and tax you—he'll take the best of your fields, your vineyards, and your flocks. You shall be his slaves. Just like it was back in Egypt. And then you'll cry to the Lord for help. But the Lord won't help you this time. Do you still want a king?" (see 1 Samuel 8:11–18).

"We want a king! We want a king! We want a king!" The people reject their special relationship of having God as king and willingly choose to return to having a human lord—a pharaoh, if you will—but just a human lord who is "one of them" rather than a foreigner.

> CHAPTER 5, OPTIONAL QUEST #5: READ 1 SAMUEL 10–31 (COMPLETE QUEST AND LEVEL UP TO OT HISTORIAN, HONORS GRADUATE AWARD).

So God sends Samuel to anoint Saul as Israel's first king. God speaks these words through Samuel: "I brought up Israel out of Egypt, I rested you from the hand of the Egyptians and from the hand of all the kingdoms that were oppressing you. But today you have rejected your God" (1 Samuel 10:18–19). So the question now is: Led by a king, can both the people and the king serve the Lord? Spoiler: No.

King Saul's reign is complicated. On the one hand, he stabilizes the country, bringing some order. But he loves war. He sometimes doesn't know where his role ends and the roles of the prophets and priests start. Saul also seems to fall into mental illness and become unstable.

God's eyes—and the eyes of many in Israel—turn to a young man from Bethlehem named David, son of Jesse, son of Obed, son of Ruth, daughter-in-law of Naomi.

God says to Samuel, "I regret that I have made Saul king, for he has turned away from following me and has not carried out my words" (1 Samuel 15:11). And so God breaks up with Saul and sends Samuel to anoint David as king.

The anointing of David is one of the most wonderful stories in the Old Testament. The words *see* and *say* are

Luckily in a democracy we have elections and term limits to keep mentally unstable war mongers out of office . . . theoretically.

THE BISHOP

important to the story. Jesse of Bethlehem lines up his seven oldest sons from oldest to youngest for Samuel to consider. Because God says to Samuel, "I have *seen* a king for myself among his sons. . . . I will let you know what to do, you shall anoint the one I *say* to." So Samuel *looks* upon the eldest son, Eliab, and *says* to himself, "Surely this is the Lord's anointed!" But God *says*, "Do not *look* upon his appearance, for the Lord does not *see* as humans *see*; they *look* on the outward appearance, but the Lord *looks* upon the heart." So Jesse brings up his son Abinadab, and then Shammah. "The Lord has not chosen either of these," Samuel says. Jesse brings each of his seven oldest boys forward, but none of them are to be anointed king. "Are all your sons here?" "Well, the youngest is out keeping watch over the flock."

CUE THE MUSIC! CUT TO DAVID WITH THE SHEEP!! Remember back when God spoke to Moses in the burning-but-not-consumed bush? What was Moses doing? Keeping watch over the flock. That is what God's servants do—they tend God's flock. And sure enough! David comes in and Samuel says, "Anoint him immediately! He is the one!"

The rest of the book of 1 Samuel is a long and strange trip. David plays a mean bluegrass guitar, which Saul kind of digs. David defeats the mighty Goliath and becomes the best friend of Saul's son Jonathan—the two pinkie-swear to be BFFs. David rises in the service of Saul and Israel. But Saul descends into madness and grows jealous of David. Saul seeks to have David murdered, but Jonathan helps David. One day, when Saul is hunting for David, David hides in a cave. Saul comes into the cave to take a leak. David has respect for the office of king, so rather than kill Saul, David pulls out his knife and slices off a corner of Saul's shirt. For a while, David has to flee the country, and he actually takes service with the Philistine king Achish. After David leaves the Philistines, they come up to battle Israel. Israel is defeated and both Saul and Jonathan are slain. David is then the undisputed king of Israel. It's messy.

King David—A Seriously Hot Mess (2 Samuel)

> CHAPTER 5, OPTIONAL QUEST #6: READ 2 SAMUEL (COMPLETE QUEST AND LEVEL UP TO OT HISTORIAN, MASTERS LEVEL).

It is really hard to figure out the David story. The name of David is mentioned more times in the Old Testament than any other human. More than Moses. More than Abraham. More than Isaiah. More even than Ichabod or Maher-Shalal-Hash-baz. Although Moses's story lasts for more chapters, David's narrative is actually longer, since most of Moses's chapters are comprised of laws and rituals. Abraham and Sarah were the founders of the people; Moses was the law giver, deliverer, and covenant maker;

but David is the kingdom builder. The one who fashions the tribes into a nation. His accomplishments in battle, in art, in kingdom building and faith raise him to one of the great figures in the human story.

On the other hand, David is a hot mess. Far from being a servant king who tends God's flock with the care of a shepherd, David's life is shambolic. In Charles Barkley's words, David is not a role model.

Some readers interpret David as a strong king—the best king Israel ever had. True, David does many good things. He is loyal to King Saul to a certain degree—twice foregoing the chance to slay him. He does not openly rebel against Saul or lead an insurrection. He is loyal to his friend Jonathan. David slays Goliath with his speed, accuracy, and guile. He is remembered as a great poet, singer, and artist. David unifies the twelve tribes by moving the capital to Jerusalem. He then brings the ark of the covenant to Jerusalem—symbolically and physically placing God at the center of the people. David subdues Israel's neighbors, and the people have relative security during his life. At times, David shows mercy to his enemies when he defeats them. All future Judean kings are compared to David—and almost all of them are found wanting.

Some readers interpret David as no better than, as a friend of mine says, "the worst warlord in Mogadishu." David is a warrior who revels in battle and bloodshed. The saying goes, "Saul has killed his thousands, and David his ten thousands." While David chooses to show mercy at certain points, on other occasions he is ruthless and merciless. But sometimes the mercy he shows is unwise—maybe even cruel. For example, Saul first gives his daughter Michal to David to marry. But when David and Saul come to oppose each other, Saul gives Michal to another man, who loves her. To consolidate his kingdom, David insists that Michal be returned to him. But he never loves her, and she dies childless.

THE ELDER

I am confident that an HBO series on the life of David would rock. Who needs a dragon or white walkers when you have the man after God's own heart?

An even more telling example is the rape of Tamar. David has children by many different wives. David's firstborn son is Amnon—whose mother is Ahinoam. By a woman named Maacah, David has a daughter Tamar and a son Absalom. Ammon rapes his half-sister Tamar (2 Samuel 13). But David refuses to punish Amnon, because David loves him. David proves too weak of a father to punish his son. [Nice parenting, you weak father—Tamar deserved better from you!] This reminds us of Eli, who was too weak to punish his sons. I guess kings are no better than priests or prophets or judges. When David refuses to punish Amnon, Absalom takes it into his own hands to avenge his sister—and Absalom has Amnon executed. Once again, David is too weak to punish Absalom adequately. David allows Absalom to live in Jerusalem, but Absalom is not allowed into David's presence.

After a few years, Absalom leads a revolt against David. He gathers disgruntled lords and soldiers, and they drive David out of Jerusalem. David regains the throne, but in the battle that ensues, Absalom is killed.

And then there is David's most embarrassing sin, a sin that is on the cover of the tabloids for two generations. One spring, David decides not to lead his armies to war. Instead, gazing over the Jerusalem rooftops from his palace, he sees a beautiful woman named Bathsheba. Problem: Bathsheba is married to Uriah, who is a captain in David's army. David doesn't care. Long story short: David and Bathsheba have sex. Bathsheba gets pregnant. To cover it up, David arranges for Uriah and the company he captains to be abandoned in battle—they all die. David pretends to be a just king, taking in and caring for the widow of his loyal soldier. The prophet Nathan confronts David—and to his credit, the king admits guilt, repents, and seeks God's mercy.

2 Samuel 7 describes the covenant God makes with David. So far, we have seen God's covenant through Noah—the promise never again to seek to destroy the creation. Then there was God's covenant with Abraham and Sarah—the promise of a land, descendants who would be

---

Let me guess, David popped a tic-tac and told the soldiers that fetched Bathsheba that

THE ACOLYTE

the ladies love his attention because he's so powerful . . .

a great nation with a great name, and to be a blessed people through whom God would bless others. Third came the covenant with Moses at Sinai—I will be your God, you will be my priestly people, blessing other nations. The covenant in 2 Samuel 7 plays with the Hebrew word for *house*—which can mean a house for humans, a house of worship for God, or a dynasty for a king (as in the "house of Windsor"). When he moves to Jerusalem, David builds himself a house (his palace). After moving in, he decides that he should build the Lord a house (a temple). But God says, "No, I will build *you* a house [a dynasty]. Your son will build me a house [a temple]. One of your descendants will forever be the anointed, the messiah, the king. He shall call me father and I will call him son." Many centuries later, Jesus the Son of God taught us all to pray, "Our Father, who art in heaven . . ."

So what do you think, O faithful reader? Was David a faithful king? Was he a faithless thug? Do his accomplishments merit our praise? Or does his wagonload of flaws deserve judgment? Did he prove to be a "man after God's own heart"? Maybe he was just sort of like all of us—a mixed bag, with some hateable qualities and some lovable qualities. A sinner and a saint at the same time.

Kings and Prophets—A Necessary Check and Balance

The rise of dynastic kingship in Israel necessitated a corrective, countering institution to serve as a check and balance on the power and primacy of the kings. The institution that God used was prophecy. The age of kingship in Israel—about 1040–587 BCE—was also the golden age of Old Testament prophecy.

It is true that there were prophets prior to the advent of the monarchy. Abraham, Moses, Miriam, Deborah, and Balaam were prophets prior to kingship. The institution of prophecy already existed. But with the rise of the monarchy, the institution of prophecy took on a much greater importance. The power and privilege of the monarchy—if left unchecked—inevitably leads to oppression and to ruin.

The prophets had several important roles to play to check and balance the monarchy.

First, the prophets *anointed* new kings—thus serving both to validate the new king and to authorize his rule. Conversely, if a prophet did not anoint the new king, the king's reign might be seen as invalid.

Second, the prophets were God's messengers, delivering God's words to the king, the country, and the people. This was really the main role of the prophets—to be God's messengers who spoke God's word. The prophets often introduced or concluded their messages with some sort of "messenger formula," identifying God as the true speaker of the message. They would say, "Thus says the Lord," or "An oracle of the Lord," or "Hear the word of the Lord." The prophets were surrounded by groups of followers— faithful disciples who recorded the prophets' words and preserved them for future generations.

Third, the prophets interpreted and applied the religious tradition to new times and situations. As the centuries passed, the beginnings of Israel's sacred Scriptures emerged. The authoritative laws of Moses and the Mosaic tradition grew. The words of the prophets were collected and copied and preserved. The prophets applied these nascent sacred traditions to new generations. The kings were expected to be faithful to God and the divine tradition. The prophets were to interpret the tradition for the king. Very often, the king would consult with a prophet to see if a particular course of action was God's will. This was called "inquiring of the Lord" or "seeking the Lord."

THE DEACON

Fourth, prophets left cryptic clues no one understood then about contemporary geopolitics. Ugh.

Many people think of the prophets as messengers of judgment—calling for justice and announcing doom. But the prophets spoke words of hope and deliverance just as often as they did messages of judgment. The prophet discerned the word of the Lord for the current moment. Then the prophet spoke that word with imagination and purpose. They spoke against injustice. But their words also called hope and courage into existence. In terms of the kings, when a king despairs and loses hope, he might inhabit dangerous behaviors. So speaking words of hope was often the prophet's best way to curb the worst impulses of the monarchy.

Solomon—The King Israel Said They Wanted (1 Kings 1–11)

CHAPTER 5, OPTIONAL QUEST #7: READ 1 KINGS 1–11 (COMPLETE QUEST AND

LEVEL UP TO OT HISTORIAN, DOC-
TORAL LEVEL).

When the people demanded a king—"We want a king!
We want a king!"—God had Samuel warn the people
what kings were good for: "A king will take your sons
and force them to be soldiers in his armies and workers
for his massive building projects—like building himself
a huge palace. He will take your daughters to serve as his
sex toys, his cooks, and his cleaners. He will tax you and
tax you—he'll take the best of your fields, your vineyards,
and your flocks. You shall be his slaves."

After David dies, there is a struggle to see who will
succeed him. Bathsheba—the same one who had the affair
with David and whose husband David had murdered—
becomes the force who sees that the crown passes to her
son Solomon. Solomon becomes the exact king that Samuel warned they would get.

On the one hand, Solomon shows some wisdom. Solomon prays for wisdom, and he seems to show great wisdom when judging legal disputes between other parties
(see 1 Kings 3). He constructs the temple for the Lord that
David had wished to build. He orders massive fortifica-
tions built and expands the military. He attracts favorable
attention from foreign dignitaries, such as the queen of
Sheba.

But when it comes to making wise decisions about
national policy, "he chose . . . poorly." His massive building projects and military expansion sorely test the economy
of the country—the taxes and forced labor are a cruel burden on the people. He marries many foreign wives, and he
accommodates their religions—allowing worship sites for

THE DEACON

Do you know where
Solomon's temple was
located? On the side of
his head.

the gods of his wives, which draws his heart away from
God. The Bible says, "Solomon did what was evil in the
eyes of the Lord, and did not completely follow the Lord" (1
Kings 11:6). And speaking of crushing taxes, check out how
much food Solomon's court requires to get by for one day:

> Solomon's provision for one day was 188 bushels
> of choice flour, and 375 bushels of meal, ten fat
> oxen, and twenty pasture-fed cattle, one hundred
> sheep, besides deer, gazelles, roebucks, and fatted
> fowl. (1 Kings 4:22–23)

And each one of those oxen, cows, sheep, and chickens
comes from the offering (tax) that Solomon requires from
his people—who are barely living above the subsistence
level.

The Holy, Unholy Rebellion—The Divided
Monarchy, 922–722 BCE (1 Kings 12–2 Kings 17)

When Solomon dies in the year 922 BCE, the northern ten
tribes—Asher, Dan, Ephraim, Gad, Issachar, Manasseh,
Naphtali, Reuben, Simeon, and Zebulun—come to his
son Rehoboam and ask him to lower their taxes (1 Kings

12). There has always been a natural division between the northern ten tribes and the southern tribe of Judah. There are ethnic, geographic, and theological differences. King David had to be crowned once in Judah and another time before all Israel at Hebron.

So when Rehoboam goes to Shechem to be crowned by all Israel, a rebel named Jeroboam speaks for the northern tribes: "Lower our taxes and we will serve you. If not, we will rebel." Rehoboam's older and wiser counselors say, "This is a good idea." But Rehoboam's younger, hothead posse says, "Hell to the no! Tell them you've got a big penis and raise their taxes!" (Really, that's what they said—I'm not editorializing.) So Rehoboam says to the northern tribes, "You think my dad's taxes were high? You are going to: Feel. My. Wrath."

This sounds too much like a presidential debate with Little Jeroboam and big-hands Rehoboam.

THE ACOLYTE

So the northern ten tribes rebel. They form their own country—Israel. The southern tribes of Judah and Benjamin stay loyal to Rehoboam.

The Bible presents this rebellion paradoxically. On the one hand, it says that the rebellion is the holy will of God because Rehoboam is so immature and unwise— "this thing is from me" (1 Kings 12:24). But the text also says that the rebellion is an unholy act of unfaithfulness, because the northern tribes are disloyal to the Davidic covenant and because Rehoboam sets up golden calves in two temples—one in Bethel and the other in Dan. He does this because he fears the religious influence that the temple in Jerusalem might have on the people. The setting up of golden calves and two rivals temples is forever seen as "the sin of Rehoboam"—the unholy act for which the entire country is later judged.

No Money for Maps: It would be cool to have a map showing the division of the land into the divided monarchy. But there's no money for maps—so Google it or open a nice study Bible.

For the next two hundred years—from 922 to 722 BCE—the people of God exist as two separate kingdoms. The Northern Kingdom, Israel, enjoys certain advantages—it is more populous, more prosperous, has more and better agricultural land, and has more access to trade. But the country is inherently unstable. One rebellion often leads to another, when the first rebels are crowned and discover that "it's good to be the king." The Northern Kingdom is plagued by short-lived dynasties and many rebellions—at one point having three kings in a single year.

The Southern Kingdom, Judah, is less populated and prosperous, but they have the stable Davidic monarchy, the capital of Jerusalem with its walls and temple, and rugged mountain lands, making them more difficult to invade or conquer. The two countries are often at odds, with the Northern Kingdom at times dominated by or going to war with the Southern Kingdom. But in the end, the Northern Kingdom is conquered first, falling to Assyria in 722 BCE.

The Kings and Their Prophetic Pesterers

King Ahab of Israel marries a foreign woman, Jezebel, who brings with her the worship of the pagan gods Baal and Asherah. Ahab is one of the most powerful and successful kings of Israel—we know this from extrabiblical sources and archaeology. But God raises up prophets to speak against the powerful king Ahab and Jezebel. God sends them to call Israel back to faithfulness and to speak hope into existence. The prophet Elijah is the greatest of these prophets. His greatest moment is a confrontation with 450 prophets of Baal at Mount Carmel. It's one prophet of the Lord versus 450 of Baal's. It is Baal's home stadium. Baal gets to swing first. And the choice of weapons is Baal's. Baal is the god of the thunderstorm, so the contest is who can call down lightning from heaven first. Ahab calls Elijah a "pesterer of Israel." Elijah says, "Let Israel decide today whom they will serve—the Lord or Baal. Quit limping along—you cannot follow both. Choose." On that day, the Lord proves faithful, and Elijah prevails.

Jeroboam II is another very successful and powerful king of Israel. During his reign, the country seems prosperous but there is a spiritual rot at the heart of the people. God sends the prophet Amos to "roar" from Zion in Jerusalem. To call down judgment and speak hope into existence. Amos says that Israel and Judah are just as unrighteous as all the pagan countries around them—but they have no excuse because they have the word of the Lord. Amos says Samaria, the capital of Israel, and Israel's sacred worship sites of Bethel and Gilgal are actually sites of unholy worship. "Go to Bethel and Gilgal to bring your offerings, but the only thing that you are actually doing there is multiplying your own sin!" (Amos 4:4). Amos says their courts are corrupt, the poor are oppressed and fleeced, and people hope in God—but God is going to send judgment not salvation. He famously says that God wants not rote ritual worship but the living faith of obedient followers:

> I hate, I despise your festivals,
>> and I take no delight in your solemn
>> assemblies.
> . . . .
> Let justice roll down like waters,
>> and righteousness like an everflowing
>> stream. (Amos 5:21–24)

After Amos, the prophet Hosea speaks God's word to the Northern Kingdom. Under a bewildering series of kings—Jeroboam, Zachariah, Shallum, Menachem, Pekahiah, Pekah, and Hosea—Hosea preaches God's word over many years. His prophetic ministry sees the destruction of the Northern Kingdom. On the one hand, Hosea accuses the people of being unfaithful to God. "Like a woman who is unfaithful to her husband, you are unfaithful to God," says Hosea. He says that the people have abandoned God's basic law:

> There is no faithfulness or faithful love,
>> and no knowledge of God in the land.
> Swearing, lying, and murder,
>> stealing and adultery break out.
> Bloodshed follows bloodshed (Hosea 4:1–2)

Hosea witnesses the destruction of the Northern Kingdom, but he also sees that there is hope—because God is alive and the God of the living. Here, I follow the translation of the NRSV; God is portrayed as the loving parent who cannot let the beloved child go away.

> When Israel was a child, I loved him,
> > and out of Egypt I called my son.
> . . . .
> My heart recoils within me;
> > my compassion grows warm and tender.
> I will not execute my fierce anger;
> > I will not again destroy Ephraim;
> for I am God and no mortal,
> > the Holy One in your midst,
> > and I will not come in wrath. (Hosea 11:1,
> > > 8–9)

The Northern Kingdom is conquered in 722, and the people are sent into exile and don't survive as a nation. Wherever they are sent, they marry into the local populations and disappear into the mists of history—but many of the refugees of the Northern Kingdom flee south, where they join Judah and reunite with the Davidic line and the people of Jerusalem. The books of 1–2 Kings blame the Northern Kingdom's fall on Israel's rebellion against David and the worship of the golden calves at Dan and Bethel. Amos and Hosea say that the fall is called by their unrighteousness—failing to worship only God and to love the neighbor by leading lives of justice and service.

Meanwhile in the Southern Kingdom of Judah, the great prophet Isaiah arises, speaking God's word to many kings over many years. The prophet Micah also preaches to Judah at the same time. During these years, the Northern Kingdom of Israel first attacks Judah and then wars with the empire of Assyria, falling in 722. Assyria also wages war against Judah and Jerusalem—but is unable to fully conquer Jerusalem. Micah and Isaiah both call for the people to be faithful to God and to live lives of righteousness and justice. It is possible here only to give the smallest sample of the great feast of words and ideas in the poetry of Isaiah and Micah. Isaiah sings:

> Wash yourselves; make yourselves clean;
>> remove the evil of your doings
>> from before my eyes;
> cease to do evil,
>> learn to do good;
> seek justice,
>> rescue the oppressed,
> defend the orphan,
>> plead for the widow. (Isaiah 1:16–17 NRSV)

Micah famously says:

> With what shall I come before the Lord,
>> and bow myself before God on high?
> Shall I come before him with burnt offerings,
>> with calves a year old?
> Will the Lord be pleased with thousands of rams,
>> with ten thousands of rivers of oil?
> Shall I give my firstborn child for my
>> transgression,
>> the fruit of my body for the sin of my soul?
> He has told you, O human, what is good!
>> What does the Lord require of you?
> Do justice, love faithfulness,
>> and walk intentionally with your God!
>> (Micah 6:6–8)

Micah preaches these words even as the very kings of Judah—under pressure from Assyria—commit child sacrifice! The very thing Micah says is unthinkable. King Ahaz "made his son pass through the fire" (2 Kings 16:3). And King Manasseh sheds more blood in Jerusalem than any other king.

In the midst of the great evil in the city, in the midst of attacks from foreign kingdoms and empires, Isaiah speaks hope into existence. God will not abandon God's people—God will save the people. Isaiah also promises that God will be faithful to the promise to David: that one of David's descendants—who will come to be called *Messiah* (which means *anointed one*)—will one day come. Isaiah probably thinks that King Hezekiah is the one to come. Remember that Jesse was David's father; here Isaiah speaks about David's family tree: "A shoot shall come out from the stump of Jesse, and a branch shall grow out of his roots" (Isaiah 11:1).

Micah promises that the ideal Davidic king will one day be born in "Bethlehem of Ephrathah." Yet, Micah also says that one day Jerusalem itself will fall, because its sins

---

I love the image of speaking hope into existence. Too often our imaginations

THE BISHOP

are determined by the landscape of our situation and need, not by the soundscape of God.

are as great as those of the Northern Kingdom. "What is the transgression of Jacob? Is it not Samaria? And what is the high place of Judah? Is it not Jerusalem?" (Micah 1:5). A *high place* is an unauthorized worship site, where Micah believes evil practices are committed. And yet both prophets, in nearly identical prophetic messages, speak hope of peace and deliverance into existence. People will come from all of the nations to be blessed by the word of the Lord of Israel:

> "Come, let us go up to the mountain of the Lord,
>   to the house of the God of Jacob;
> that he may teach us his ways."
> . . . .
> They shall beat their swords into plowshares,
>   and their spears into pruning hooks;
> nation shall not lift up sword against nation,
>   neither shall they learn war any more.
>   (Micah 4:2–3; Isaiah 2:3–4)

The words of those prophets are carved today into the statue of a man beating his sword into a plow. The statue stands in front of the United Nations.

The final 150 years of the nation of Judah see more of the same. The people and kings prove that the words of Joshua were true. They cannot serve the Lord. The cannot perfectly love either God or their neighbor. They cannot avoid sin and injustice.

The prophet Jeremiah urges the people with creative and powerful preaching, condemning their unfaithfulness and urging them to return to God. In his most famous sermon, Jeremiah goes to the temple and tells the people not to trust in the empty promise that God will protect Jerusalem and its holy temple.

But if you truly make better your ways and your actions, if you truly act justly to another, if you do not oppress the immigrant, the orphan, and the widow, or spill innocent blood in this place. If you do not go after other gods to your own hurt, then I will dwell with you in this place, in the land that I gave of old to your ancestors forever and ever. But here you are, trusting in deceptive words to no avail. Will you steal, murder, commit adultery, swear falsely, make offerings to Baal, and go after other gods that you have not known, and then come and stand before me in this house, which is called by my name, and say, "It's all good!"—only to go on doing all these abominations? (Jeremiah 7:5–10)

King Josiah is crowned and attempts to reform the nation and bring the people back to the Lord. He remodels the temple and, in the process, discovers an ancient copy of Deuteronomy. After the book is read to him, he attempts to reform the nation according to the laws and truths in that book. But it's hopeless. The people cannot serve the Lord. In 609, Josiah is killed by Pharaoh Neco.

Shortly after that, the Babylonian Empire conquers Assyria, defeats Egypt, and destroys Jerusalem. The Babylonians deport Judah's leading citizens into exile in two waves—the first deportation occurs in 597 and the second deportation after the destruction of Jerusalem in 587. Many other of God's people flee elsewhere—some to Egypt, others to Damascus, others further in to Africa or up toward Asia and Europe. King Jehoiachin is deported to Babylon in the first wave. Several years into his exile, he is released from prison and given a monthly paycheck by the king. He is invited into the emperor's presence—his shame is removed, and he is given a place of honor by the emperor.

No Money for Maps: Yeah, for a map of Judah's Babylonian exile, just Google it or open up a good Study Bible.

One thing becomes clear: Israel cannot serve the Lord. They couldn't do it when they were organized loosely by tribes and led by judges. They couldn't do it when they were led by kings, with prophets to serve as checks and balances on royal prerogative. Israel cannot serve the Lord.

The question then is simple: What is God going to do about a people who can't serve the Lord, but whom God has claimed by means of the divine promise? What is God going to do—that becomes the question.

In Exile—A Promise of Restoration and Hope (597/587–539 BCE)

In exile, the people think that they have been cut off from the Lord and that they have no hope. Listen to the complaints of the people in exile:

> My way is hidden from the Lord,
>   and my rightful cause is disregarded by my
>   God. (Isaiah 40:27)

> Our bones are dried up, and our hope is lost; we are completely cut off [from God]. (Ezekiel 37:11)

> Our captors mocked us, our tormentors teased us saying, "Sing us one of those songs about Mount Zion!" (Psalm 137:3)

Before you say that they sound like a bunch of whiners—remember that life in exile really sucks. Your whole identity gone. Your country. Your land. Your people. Your religious house. Your actual house. Your loved ones. All gone—most of them destroyed or forced into exile.

Almost your entire identity gone and dead. Almost. But almost gone and dead is the same as a little alive. Because the Judeans in exile have two things going for them. They still know their story—the story of God's unfathomable faithfulness to God's promises. And they still have God.

In exile, God raises up prophets to speak hope into existence. In Egypt, the old prophet Jeremiah is still at work preaching the word of God. When the Babylonian armies came for the last time, Jeremiah's disciples forced him to flee to Egypt—even though he wanted to stay. In Babylon, there is a young priest named Ezekiel who had been deported in the first wave in 597. God reaches out across the many miles and calls him to be a prophet of hope. Also in Babylon is a prophet whose name has been lost, but we know his or her writings—they were added to the book of Isaiah. We call this prophet Second Isaiah—these writings of hope can be found in Isaiah 40–55. Listen to the words, through which they preached hope into existence:

Jeremiah:

> "The days are surely coming," says the Lord, "when I will make a new covenant with the house of Israel and the house of Judah. It will not be like the covenant that I made with their

ancestors when I took them by the hand to bring them out of the land of Egypt—a covenant that they broke, though I was their lord," says the Lord. "But this is the covenant that I will make with the house of Israel. . . . I will put my law within them, and I will write it on their hearts; and I will be their God, and they shall be my people." (Jeremiah 31:31–33)

Ezekiel:

For thus says the Lord God, "I my very self will seek for my sheep, and will find them. As shepherds seek out their flocks when they are among their scattered sheep, so I will seek out my sheep. I will rescue them. . . . I will provide for them on good pasture, and the mountain heights of Israel shall be their pasture; there they shall lie down in good grazing land, and they shall feed on rich pasture on the mountains of Israel. I myself will be the shepherd of my sheep, and I will give them rest," says the Lord God. (Ezekiel 34:11–15)

Second Isaiah:

Now the Lord says—
    who formed me in the womb to be his
        servant,
to bring Jacob back to him,
    and that Israel might be gathered to him,
. . . .
"It is too insignificant a thing that you should be
    my servant

> merely to raise up the tribes of Jacob
> and to restore the survivors of Israel;
> I will give you as a light to the nations,
> that my salvation may reach to the end of
> the earth." (Isaiah 49:5–6)

The miraculous thing that God does is that God once again proves faithful to the divine promises to Abraham and Sarah, to Moses and Miriam, to David and his children. Through the preaching of the prophets, God speaks hope into existence.

After their long history from slavery in Egypt to exile in Babylon, I would understand the people of God having some cynical ears.

THE ELDER

But notice especially the call of Second Isaiah back to the missional purpose of God for God's people. They are blessed to be a blessing to other people. "It is too insignificant a thing . . . to restore the survivors of Israel; I will give you as a light to the nations." Elsewhere in Second Isaiah, the prophet says, "I have given you as a covenant to the people, a light to the nations" (Isaiah 42:6). God is renewing the people not just physically but also spiritually—renewing them for the sake of God's mission to love, save, and bless the whole earth.

Returned but Not Returned—God's Holy People after the Exile (539 BCE and after; Ezra, Nehemiah, Malachi)

In 539 BCE, the Babylonians are conquered by the Persians, and God's people—along with all of the other conquered people the Babylonians had forced into exile—are allowed to return home.

After they return home, they rebuild the temple and they worship God there. The old folks—who had been kids in 587 when the temple was destroyed and who remember the glories of Solomon's Temple—weep when they see the new temple.

But not all of God's people return. Some of God's people follow the advice that Jeremiah had written to them in exile before he died. Jeremiah had written: "Wherever you live, build houses and live in them; plant gardens and eat what they produce. Take wives and have sons and daughters; take wives for your sons, and give your daughters in marriage, that they may bear sons and daughters; multiply there, and do not decrease. But seek the welfare of the city where I have sent you into exile, and pray to the Lord on its behalf, for in its welfare you will find your welfare" (Jeremiah 29:5–7).

As God's covenant people, blessed to be a blessing, called to be a priestly kingdom, God's people are to seek the welfare of the society around them—no matter where God puts them. They are to seek the prosperity of the city around them. For in that prosperity, they will find their own prosperity.

So not all of the exiled citizens of Judah return home. Many stay where they are and live out their lives of covenant service—blessing others around them, seeking the prosperity and peace of the cities where they live, acting as God's priestly people.

At this point in the Old Testament story, we can start to call God's people *Jews*. Until now, they have been Hebrews or Israelites or Judeans. Now we can start to call them Jews—they are the descendants of the kingdom of Judah.

A profound change takes place in God's people at this time. Because they are no longer gathered in one place and also because they are no longer an independent nation—but are now a province in the Persian Empire—their nature fundamentally changes.

Rather than being a holy nation with a king to lead them, they become a holy people with priests to lead them. Rather than having a Holy Land to live in with a holy temple at their center, they center their lives around a holy book (Israel's Scriptures). Rather than having national boundaries, they develop religious boundaries. In short, they become a people of the book, following holy practices centered in God's word, who are led by priests and scribes and scriptural experts. If they had tried to rebel against Persia—as they do later against Rome—they would have been crushed (as the Romans do crush them). The people discern that God is calling them to seek to serve God as a people, as a religion rather than a nation, with the holy word at their center rather than a holy kingdom.

As they live into this new identity, the office of prophecy slowly recedes in importance. The office of prophet, after all, had mainly grown important in response to kingship. Judah no longer has her own king, so the check-and-balance power of the prophet is no longer as important.

But God's people have learned to trust in God. To believe that God will find a way—somehow and some impossible way—to keep the divine promises to Abraham and Sarah, to Jacob and Rachel, to Moses and Miriam and David. So they cling to the hope that God will indeed one day send an ideal Davidic descendant—the anointed one, the messiah.

Until that happened, they would live out a new faith experiment. Could Judah serve the Lord as a religious people, a holy people devoted to the word and led by priests and scribes, rather than by prophets, judges, or kings.

What shape would God's faithfulness to God's promises and God's people take in the future?

6

Mourning into Dancing, or How to Get in God's Face

This book has focused on the narrative arc of the Old Testament. In particular, I've developed an argument that the God of the Old Testament is a God who is both faithful and holy. God is faithful to the beloved creation—sustaining it and committed to its redemption and rescue. God is on a mission to love, save, bless, and redeem the entire creation. Toward that mission, God elected Abraham, Sarah, and their descendants—Israel—to be a priestly people, blessed in order that through them God might bless, save, and ultimately redeem all the families of the earth. God is faithful to the divine promises to Israel—finding seemingly impossible ways to keep those divine promises from generation to generation.

God is also a holy and in-your-face God. Not content either to abandon the broken creation or to remain distant and uninvolved from the creation, God gets deeply involved with creation—especially with humanity, who alone are created in the very image of God. Through the law, God gets right up in humanity's grill—working through the law to give birth to a more trustworthy creation, a creation in which life can flourish. But God's people, in the end, cannot adequately serve, be loyal to, or be faithful to this intensely holy God. As Joshua announces, "You cannot serve the Lord!" And this prediction proved prophetically true. As individuals, we cannot serve the Lord. As a loose confederacy, organized by tribes and led by judges and directly ruled by God, we cannot serve the Lord. As a singular kingdom, united under one powerful king, we cannot serve. As divided kingdoms, with kings ruling and prophets serving to critique and curb the king's prerogative, we cannot serve the Lord. And yet God is faithful—staying true to the divine commitment to God's people.

That has been the argument of this book—an argument based on the narrative history of biblical Israel as recounted from Genesis through 2 Kings and beyond to Ezra and Nehemiah. With the prophetic witness of Amos, Hosea, Isaiah, Micah, Jeremiah, Ezekiel, and Second Isaiah providing essential context and corrective.[1]

Israel's Poetry of Faith

But as I expressed in chapter 1, the spiritual library that is the Old Testament contains more than just narrative, law, and prophecy. It also contains poetry. The Old Testament contains the poetry of faith. This poetry of faith is found in two major groups—the psalms and the wisdom literature

(Proverbs, Ecclesiastes, Job). (Lamentations contains lament psalms, as the title suggests, while the Song of Songs contains erotic lyrical poetry.) In this chapter, there's only space to consider the psalms, which have been the most important form of Israel's poetry for the worship lives and personal faith lives of God's people across the centuries. I commend the wisdom literature, Song of Songs, and Lamentations to the reader for further study.

It is here where the historical distance between us and the people of Israel is most easily collapsed.

THE BISHOP

The book of Psalms contains 150 faith poems of various types. There are hymns of praise, cries for help, prayers of trust, songs of thanksgiving, wisdom psalms, liturgies, and more. Here, I will introduce briefly only the major types of psalms.

Like a Tree Walking Down the Road—Psalm 1 (Wisdom Psalms)

Psalms is filled with images. And the first two images in the Psalter are that of a road that forks into two and that of a tree. One part *Wizard of Oz* and one part *Lord of the Rings*, the poem invites you to picture yourself as a tree walking down a yellow-bricked road. But rather than leading to a crackpot wizard, this road leads to God. Hey, this is poetry! If you want a tree that walks, that's just fine:

> Enviable is the one who does
>> not walk in the advice of the wicked,
>> not stand on the road of sinners, and
>> not sit in the seat of scoffers.
> But who delights in the law of the Lord,
>> and chews on God's law, day and night.
> This one is like a tree
>> planted by streams of water,
> which yields fruit in each season,
>> whose leaves do not wither.
> In all that it does, its flourishes.
>
> Not so the wicked!
>> They are like chaff that the wind drives
>> away.
> Therefore the wicked will not stand in the
>> tough times,
>> nor sinners in the congregation of the
>> righteous;
> For the Lord watches over the way of the
>> righteous,
>> but the way of the wicked leads to destruc-
>> tion. (Psalm 1)

The two roads signal the directions one takes in life. But the roads are characterized not by their geography ("you take the high road, and I'll take the low road") but rather by who walks on each road and to whom each road belongs. Down one road walks the wicked (those who do not depend on God), the sinners (those who rebel against God's will), and the scoffers (those who mock God). Notice the great poetry: do not walk, stand, or sit with the wicked. This road belongs to those who tread its path. This road leads nowhere. Those who take this road end up being non-resilient—they cannot take suffering. Down the other road walks the righteous (those who depend on God). This other road belongs not to those who take it but to God—who watches over it.

The other picture in Psalm 1 is of a tree. Those who depend on God (the righteous) are like a tree whose roots are sunk deep into the earth next to a flowing stream. Because of this, the tree can flourish—even in dry seasons, even when the going gets tough. Like this tree, which drinks deeply from streams of water, the righteous who rely on God also drink daily from the Torah—from God's word. They are resilient, but God watches over the paths they walk.

Psalm 1 introduces the entire book of Psalms and says that the psalms are "Torah." Psalm 1 makes a promise about the psalms: those who drink deeply from them will find a sustainable source of spiritual drink. A source that sustains one on the road of life and a source that will never run dry.

Music connection: Consider the difference between an anthem to American individualism and Psalm 1. "My Way," made popular by Frank Sinatra, says "I did it my way." I trusted myself; I grasped my own destiny. Psalm 1 says, "There is a better way—God's way. You don't have to trust yourself or steer your own ship. Trust God—it's better that way."

The Seated God Who Gives Seats of Honor at God's Table—Psalm 113 (Hymns of Praise)

Psalm 113 is a classic hymn of praise—perhaps we can consider it *the* classic hymn of praise—perfectly embodying the form of a praise psalm: opening call to praise (Praise the Lord!), reasons for praise (a picture of what God's work looks like), closing call to praise (Praise the Lord!).

> Praise the Lord!
>
> Praise, O servants of the Lord!
>   Praise the name of the Lord!
> Blessed be the name of the Lord
>   from this time on and forevermore.
> From the rising of the sun to its setting
>   the name of the Lord is to be praised.
> The Lord is high above all nations,
>   and his glory above the heavens.
>
> Who is like the Lord our God,
>   who is seated on high,
> who looks far down
>   on the heavens and the earth?
>
> He raises the poor man from the dust,
>   and lifts the needy man from the ash heap,
> to give him a seat of honor with princes,
>   with the princes of his people!
> Who gives the barren woman a home sitting
>   room,
>   making her the joyous mother of children.
>
> Praise the Lord!

It begins with a triune call to praise, which names the object of praise. The opening call to praise (1) names whom to praise (the Lord); (2) who is to do the praising (the servants of the Lord); and again, more specifically how to address our praise (to the name of the Lord). One important aspect here is the connection between praise and being servants of the Lord. Praise is one of the ways that we can become servants of the Lord. In the very act of praising God, we become God's own people. And the name of the Lord—YHWH—is how we address our praise. This is not generic feeling good or telling an unhearing, impersonal universe that we are grateful for life. No. Our praise is to the personal and communal God of the Bible.

God gives us God's name to use. To use in prayer. To use in praise. To use whenever we need to drop a name. The gift of God's name both offers us the object of our praise (the Lord) and promises us that our praise shall be heard (because God's name itself reveals God's faithful character).

Now that's intriguing. I wonder why I am so uncomfortable with more specific namings of the divine?

THE ACOLYTE

By way of offering reasons for praise, the psalm offers a picture of God in God's holiness and then two pictures of what it looks like when God saves. The psalm thus describes God's self-emptying, gracious intrusion into the life of creation.

The picture of God: God is enthroned in heaven (Hebrew verb here is *yashab*, which can mean *to be enthroned*, *to sit*, or *to have a house*). God is enthroned in holy heaven, far above the troubles of the earth. But the holy God is not content to be a distant, unmoved creator. Instead God looks down on the earth and sees those who suffer—the poor man and the barren woman. These two—the poor man and the poor, barren woman—typify those whom God loves: both genders—female and male—even in their suffering, even in their poverty. God is egalitarian. And being poor is not a sign of God's disfavor but simply a sign of suffering.

And what does God do? God stoops down and raises them both. Notice the trajectory of God's downward-moving, saving power.

The Lord is high above the heavens

↓

seated on high

↓

looks far down on the heavens

↓

and then . . .

↑

he raises them up

To the poor man, God gives what I translate here as a *seat of honor* (Hebrew verb: *yashab*). And to the poor, barren woman God gives what I translate here as a *home sitting room* (Hebrew verb: *yashab*). Thus, in this salvific action, God empties God's very self of the quality that distinguishes God as holy (God's sovereign *enthronedness*) and God shares it with the poor, both female and male.

Music connection: The praise of God is both something to be memorized and then something to sing spontaneously when one experiences a moment of divinely given joy. I live in Minnesota, the land of ten thousand lakes (actually close to twenty thousand, but we are not good at math). I had always wanted to own a motorboat, so when I turned forty-five I bought a used boat. I took my then six-year-old son Gunnar for his first ride in the boat one beautiful, eighty-degree day—blue sky, a few wispy clouds, and a bald eagle soaring in the sky. We got the boat out on the lake, and Gunnar—because he's a boy—asked, "How fast will this boat go?" Because I am a boy, I said, "Let's find out!" As the boat kicked up and then planed out, Gunnar felt a moment of joy in God's good creation. Feeling that joyful exhilaration, his mind searched for a memory that sounded like he felt at the moment. He stood up and started channeling Handel's *Messiah*: "Alleluia! Alleluia! Alleluia, Alleluia, Al-le-e-u-u-ia!" That is what the praise of God sounds like, and that is what it is for.

The purpose of praise is twofold. First, praise says, "Only the Lord is God." And second, praise is the way that we give God away to the neighbor. By telling others about God in joyful and thankful ways, we give God away to our neighbor.

How to Get in God's Face—Psalm 13 (Prayers for Help, or "Laments")

Psalm 13 is a prayer for when the bottom drops out. For when life in God's good creation completely sucks. Or even partially sucks. Psalm 13 is a prayer for help—which is the most common type of psalm. Roughly one-third of the psalms in the book of Psalms are prayers for help. If the purpose of praise psalms is to say that "only the Lord is God," then the purpose of prayers for help is to say to God: "Hey! How about you actually *act* like a good and gracious and powerful God *right now*!" Praise insists that God is God. Prayers for help insist that God act like God. In other words, prayers for help are the words that God gives us to get back up in God's face when God—in all God's holiness—isn't acting holy. Funny, the holier-than-us God isn't afraid of giving us words that might seem unholy to some holier-than-thou pious people.

THE ELDER

I wish this was inscribed on the door of every church! It is too easy to deny, repress, and silence the genuine laments of the people.

These psalms are cried "out of the depths" (Psalm 130:1) or when "the waters have come up to my neck" (Psalm 69:1). As such, these psalms give expression to the deepest moments of human pain.

These psalms get in God's face in a way that claims the promise of God's presence in the midst of our suffering and also the promise that the God-who-is-with-us will preserve us from evil and bring us to a new day when the sun will rise and light will dawn. Sometimes you don't

even need the whole psalm, just a line or two. Here are
parts of Psalm 69, an important psalm for me:

> Save me, O God,
>> for the waters have come up to my neck.
> I sink in deep mire,
>> where there is no foothold;
> I have come into deep waters,
>> and the flood sweeps over me.
> I am weary with my crying;
>> my throat is parched.
> My eyes grow dim
>> with waiting for my God. (69:1–3)

Have you ever had a moment or a season in your life when
you felt like "the waters have come up to my neck"? And
I. Can't. Take. One. More. Thing. And then you get six
more damn things?

I felt like that when my second leg had to be ampu-
tated because of cancer when I was sixteen. I felt like that
when my son Gunnar needed surgery when he was both
a one-month-old and a four-month-old because he was
born with a life-threatening disease. I have felt like that
so many times in my life. Sometimes for first-world problems. Sometimes for everywhere-in-the-world problems.
Sometimes for myself or my loved ones. Sometimes for
complete strangers, neighbors who live across the street or
across the globe.

Jesus prayed a prayer like this, Psalm 22:1, when he
was being tortured to death on the psalm: "My God, my
God, why have you forsaken me?"

These psalms admit that life is not as well-ordered
as a simple Sunday-school faith may pretend. They

acknowledge that life is really messy, and they protest to heaven that things should not be as they are. And these psalms, through prayer, evoke action from God—they help move the sufferer to a new place. But these psalms also demand—demand!—that God do something. "Do something, God! Why? Because you promised! You have always been faithful to your promises, so do something."

> As for me, my prayer is to you, O Lord.
>   At an acceptable time, O God,
>   in the abundance of your steadfast love,
>   answer me.
> In your faithfulness, rescue me
>   from sinking in the mire;
> Deliver me from my enemies
>   and from the deep waters.
> Do not let the flood sweep over me,
>   or the deep swallow me up,
>   or the Pit close its mouth over me.
> Answer me, O Lord, because your steadfast love
>   is good;
>   according to your abundant mercy, turn to
>   me.
> Do not hide your face from your servant,
>   for I am in distress—make haste to answer
>   me. (69:13–17)

Notice that the reason the psalmist has the guts to get up in God's face and demand that God do something has nothing to do with the psalmist's faith or righteousness and everything to do with God's character. With God's promises: "O God, *in the abundance of your steadfast love*, answer me." And, "*In your faithfulness*, rescue me!" And, "*because your steadfast love* is good." The only thing we contribute is our need: "for I am in distress." Everything else is about God, about God's character, about our demand that God keep the divine promises of love and protection.

What a slight, but important difference, our prayers for God to come amidst our pain

THE BISHOP

and suffering are about God's character and not us.

These psalms are important for several reasons. First, they give us words for the deepest, darkest nights of our lives—when the bottom drops out, when the pain seems too much to bear. Second, these poems tell us that God is big enough for everything we've got—our pain, our anger, our questions, our doubts. Third, these psalms teach us that genuine biblical faith is comfortable challenging God. And that God is present with us precisely when it feels like God isn't there and we feel the need to get in God's face.

Music connection: Many of the most poignant songs of faith are cries for help and deliverance. The African American spirituals, "Nobody Knows the Trouble I've Seen (Nobody Knows but Jesus)," "Sometimes I Feel Like a Motherless Child," and "I am a Poor, Wayfarin'

Stranger" all give faithful witness in song to the prayers for help. Similarly, in our worship we often sing, "Lord have mercy!" Martin Luther wrote a famous song, "Out of the Depths I Cry to You," based on Psalm 130. And the blues—maybe America's greatest musical form—are a form of the prayer for help. The greatest of all blues men, B. B. King, sang, "Nobody loves me but my mama . . . and she could be jivin' too."

You Are with Me—Psalm 23 (Prayers of Trust)

The most loved psalms of all are the prayers of trust. Very similar to the prayers for help, the psalms of trust are prayed from a situation of severe crisis:

- "the valley of the shadow of death" (23:4)
- the times when "evildoers assail me" (27:2)
- the times when the "waters roar and foam" and the "mountains tremble" (46:3)
- when "the sun strikes you by day and the moon by night" (121:6)

The major difference between the prayers for help and the psalms of trust is the dominant mood. Both types of psalm depend on God. Both types of psalm at least imply a request for help. And both types of psalm include expressions of trust. But whereas the prayers for help strike the dominant note of fear and desperation, the psalms of trust hit the chord of trust. The psalms of trust confess:

- "I fear no evil, for you are with me" (23:4)
- "The Lord is my light and my salvation, whom shall I fear?" (27:1)

- "The Lord of hosts is with us, the God of Jacob is our refuge" (46:7, 11)
- "The Lord will keep you from all evil, the Lord will keep your life" (121:7)

As such, one might imagine the prayers for help as the prayers of those who are younger, who are going through their first times of crisis. The psalms of trust are the words of those who aren't riding in their first rodeo. They have been through the dark valley before, they've experienced God's steadfast love in the midst of suffering before, and they so trust—even though the dangers are very real. That is to say, these are not naïve psalms. They clearly and powerfully express the very real dangers and threats in life. And—in the midst of those dangers—they confidently express trust by means of a series of powerful metaphorical images for God: Shepherd and Table Host who gives a place of honor in the presence of enemies (23), Light and Salvation (27), Fortress and Refuge (46), Guard and Guide (121), and so on. In the end, these psalms know that "you are with me, your rod and staff they comfort me."

As such, they are the most beloved of all psalms.

Music connection: I play guitar in a bluegrass and old-time band called the Fleshpots of Egypt (based on Exodus 16:3). We lead singing in a bar once a month in Saint Paul, Minnesota, and at various other bars and worship services around Minnesota and the country. Always those two places—bars and worship services. In bars, we lead "beer and hymns," and in worship services we lead "praise and holy communion." But what we really do is sing the psalms of trust in the midst of everyday life. That's why it works so well in bars. We usually close with a medley of trust songs—"I'll Fly Away" into "May the Circle be Unbroken" into "I Saw the Light." Then we throw in a Prince song, "Purple Rain," for no reason and a Dylan song, "I Shall Be Released," because it also is a song of trust: "Any day now, any day now, I shall be released." The life of faith is about so many things. But in the end, it is about trusting in God in the highs and lows, in prosperity and scarcity, in health and sickness, when the home team wins or when you are a Vikings fan.

THE DEACON

I anticipate the day when Prince will lead the eschatological worship band. Not just because the music will rock, but the right people will be uncomfortable.

Mourning into Dancing—Psalm 30 (Songs of Thanksgiving)[2]

One of my favorite teachers, Professor James Armstrong of Princeton Theological Seminary, used to say, "We teachers don't have favorites . . . and Dave Janzen is one of them." Never Rolf Jacobson. Never Brent Strawn. Never Eunny Lee or Frank Yamada. Always ". . . and Dave Janzen is one of them."

I feel the same way about the Bible. There are so many breathtaking, earth-shattering, life-changing passages in the Scriptures, how could I possibly name one favorite passage? And each striking passage—like a single petal on a rose bush full of blossoms—is only truly beautiful in the context of the whole.

You might as well ask me to pick a favorite guitar chord—each chord is only truly meaningful as part of the progression that makes up the song and the set list.

As a student and lover of the Bible, I don't have favorite passages . . . and Psalm 30 is one of them. It is a favorite because it speaks for me. It gives me the words to sing my song.

The psalm begins with a report. The report comes in the form of a word of praise confessing an experience of divine rescue. The psalmist praises God and reports how:

> I raise you up, O Lord, for you have drawn me
> up,
> you did not let my foes rejoice over me!
> O Lord my God, I cried to you for help,
> and you healed me!
> O Lord, you lifted me right out of the earth,
> and gave me new life instead of letting me sink
> down. (Psalm 30:1–3)

Now I don't know about you, but I've been there, teetering on the edge of eternity, with one foot already buried in the ground. Or, in my case, both feet already buried.

A couple of times when I was fighting cancer as a teenager, some of the community around me pretty much gave up on my chances of making it. I didn't have favorite teachers in high school . . . and Herr Rockey, our German teacher, was one of them.

When I was first diagnosed with cancer, he came over to my house, and he gave me a gift: an ugly maroon

Gore-Tex-and-Velcro wallet, with a 5-Mark German bill in it. He said, "When you're a high-school senior, our class will go to Germany. You'll bring this wallet and this bill on the trip."

More than two years—and a great many hospitalizations and surgeries, including amputations of both my legs—later, we were on that senior-class trip to Germany. On the flight over, I beckoned him to my airplane seat, and I showed him that ugly wallet and the 5-Mark bill. I said, "Do you remember this?" We both cried. And he confessed to me, "I didn't believe it. I thought you would never make it." He, and other smart people, had almost given up on me.

THE ACOLYTE

I am crying too.

He didn't really give up on me. Not fully. My mom and dad hadn't given up on me. My sisters and brothers hadn't given up on me. My friends, the medical staff at Mayo Clinic, and my church hadn't given up on me. And God. God didn't give up on me. God pulled me through. O Lord my God, I cried to you for help and you healed me!

Following the report, the psalmist then issues an invitation. An invitation in the form of a call for the community to join the praise—"Come join the choir," the psalmist says, "lift up your voice, because God has lifted me!"

> Sing to the Lord, O his faithful ones!
> Confess! So that his holiness might be remembered!
> For his anger is momentary,
> But in his favor there is a lifetime of life!
> Weeping might overnight for an evening,
>   but in the morning: Joy!

Now this call to praise isn't just a generic, normal, harmless call to praise. You know, "Higher, higher, higher, higher, higher, higher, higher, higher, higher, lift Jesus higher!" This is a specific call to praise God because God has lifted the psalmist up from the grave. "Sing to the Lord, O his faithful ones," the psalmist cries.

"You have drawn me up," the psalmist confesses, "you lifted me right out of the earth." And because of that, he says to the community, "Sing to the Lord!"

Then the psalmist recalls both the old, pre-crisis feeling of invulnerability as well as the plunge into the depths of the crisis.

> As for me, when things were easy, I said,
>   "I'll never get shaken up."
> In your favor, O Lord,
>   you had established me as a strong
>   mountain.
> Then you hid your face;
>   I was dismayed.
> To you, O Lord, I cried,
>   and to the Lord I made supplication:
> "What profit is there in my death?
>   If I go down to the pit,
> Will the dust praise you?
>   Will it tell of your loving faithfulness?

Hear, O Lord! Show me some grace!
   O Lord, be my helper!"

It is interesting that the psalmist twice recalls what was on his or her tongue. First, there was the pre-crisis feeling that everything was going pretty well: "When things were easy, I said, 'I'll never get shaken up.'" But that was before. Before "you hid your face."

When my son Gunnar was young, he liked to play a form of the old object-permanence game most kids like to play. He would cover his face up with a blanket and ask, "Where Gunnar go?" Then he'd pull down the blanket and joyfully exclaim, "There he is!" Then—because he was two years old—he would do it again. "Where Gunnar go?" "There he is!" And again. And again.

The psalmist had experienced a reverse instance of the where-Gunnar-go-object-permanence discovery. God had always been there for the psalmist. At the right hand. In the passenger seat. Almost near enough and present enough to touch.

And then, well, God was gone. "You hid your face."

But the psalmist remembered those old Sabbath-school lessons about Moses and Miriam, Deborah and Ehud, Hannah and Samuel. About how the ancestors "cried to the Lord and the Lord heard their prayer."

So the psalmist gave it a go: "Hear, O Lord! Show me some grace!" And God did. The psalm doesn't describe in precise terms exactly what the crisis was. Maybe it was illness, or injury, or debt, or war, or deportation, or depression, or loneliness, or the death of a loved one, or crop failure, or a drought, or divorce, or a house fire.

Nor does the psalm describe what form God's grace took. Maybe it was healing, or a gift of money, or peace, or security, or rescue, or a gentle rain, or a new love. Or maybe it was a high-school German teacher coming over with an ugly gift.

Having offered a sacrifice of praise in the form of testimony, Psalm 30 closes with one of the most beautifully heart-aching sentences in the entire Bible:

> You have turned my mourning into dancing!
> > you stripped off my sackcloth and clothed
> > > me with joy,
> So that glory itself sings about you and is not
> > silent,
> > O Lord my God, I will praise you forever.

What an incredibly beautiful line: "You have turned my mourning into dancing! You stripped off my sackcloth and clothed me with joy!" I am not exactly sure how to picture that—a person "clothed with joy." But I've seen it. I've seen it in the lives of so many of God's people who God has visited with grace.

And I've lived it. I've lived a life of being clothed with joy, even as I roll around in my wheelchair with no legs, I've lived a life of mourning into dancing, a life of sackcloth-stripped-and-clothed-with-joy. If you ever meet me, you'll find me behaving with decorum, not dancing (I hope), and wearing clothes (I really, really hope). But you will also see right through those clothes—because God has stripped them off and fitted this crazy, no-legged body with a wardrobe of joy.

If the good Lord Israel ever has a business card printed up, I bet that is what it will say:

> The Lord, God of Abraham and Sarah
> > Holy and Faithful
> Mourning into Dancing
> Sackcloth into Joy

By the way. I still have that ugly maroon Gore-Tex wallet. I carry it every day. It reminds me of an important teacher in my life. And it reminds me of getting through the bad times with God's help. And it reminds me that my mourning has been turned into dancing.

Epilogue: What about the Prayer of Jabez?

In Hebrews 11, the author goes through the history of the Old Testament and describes how the great figures of Israel were able to achieve so much "by faith." Starting with Abel, who "by faith" offered "a more acceptable sacrifice" to God, the author hits the heroes of Genesis and Exodus: Noah, Abraham, Sarah, Isaac, Jacob, and Moses. Then, realizing that too much time and space have been devoted to those people, the author punts: "And what more should I say? For time would fail me to tell of Gideon, Barak, Sampson, Jephthah, of David and Samuel and the prophets . . . and women [who] received their dead by resurrection" (Hebrews 11:32–35). So the author cuts to the chase and goes right to the end of sermon.

The audience of Hebrews was probably grateful that the author skipped all those pages of his sermon and went right to the end. (Reads Hebrews 12 if you want to know the end of that sermon.)

In this short book about the Old Testament, I have to do the same thing. You might be thinking, "Hey, what about Nahum, Habakkuk, and Zephaniah? What about the Prayer of Jabez? What about Job and Ecclesiastes and the Song of Songs?"

Well, what more should I say? Time and space fail me to address all of those worthy topics—and more. I promise you that I've got a great two thousand words in me on Habakkuk and another ten thousand words on the book of Job. But there isn't time. Those worthy topics are beyond the scope of this book. I hope that I have whetted your appetite to tackle those fantastic subjects on your own. Well, maybe not the Prayer of Jabez.

This book has argued that the God of the Old Testament is a holy God and a present God—active in the world and present in people's lives. This book has also argued that the God who meets us in the Old Testament is a gracious and merciful God—above all a God who is faithful to his promises. God's word is God's bond. God keeps promises. Along that score, it is significant that the Old Testament ends with yet another a promise.

> Lo, I will send you the prophet Elijah before the great and terrible day of the Lord comes. He will turn the hearts of parents to their children and the hearts of children to their parents, so that I will not come and strike the land with a curse. (Malachi 4:5–6)

The promise is that one day, God will "turn the hearts of parents to their children and the hearts of children to their parents." In this way, the Old Testament ends by pointing to the future—to a future time when God would fulfill those promises that had not yet been kept. In particular, the Christian faith believes that the Old Testament pointed ahead to the New Testament—to the time Jesus Christ came to love, save, and redeem the world. But that is another book.

Notes

Chapter 1

1. C. S. Lewis, *The Lion, The Witch, and the Wardrobe* (Grand Rapids: Zondervan, 2005), 80–81, 191.

2. Because this is a book by a Christian written mostly for Christians and those who want to explore the Christian faith, from here on I will refer to the library of holy Hebrew books as the *Old Testament*. This is a faith commitment. I only read this holy library because of my faith in the triune God—Father, Son, and Holy Spirit. I fully respect all Jews who read and refer to this library as the Jewish Bible (the Tanak). They do so out of their own tradition and faith commitments. But for the sake of this book, I'll go with the Old Testament.

Chapter 3

1. Joseph Stein, *Fiddler on the Roof*, music by Jerry Bock, lyrics by Sheldon Harnick (New York: Limelight Editions, 1964), act 1, scene 5.

Chapter 4

1. There are some readers who wonder if Shiphrah and Puah—whose names do not sound Israelite—were actually Egyptian women who served the Israelites as midwives. I find this view unlikely for two reasons. First, the simplest translation for the Hebrew phrase describing the women is "Hebrew midwives" (not

"midwives to the Hebrews"). Second, the midwives "fear God," a designation that seems to indicate a relationship with Israel's God.

Chapter 5

1. Old Testament scholars call this portion of narrative the Deuteronomistic History (DTR), and it technically stretches from Deuteronomy through 2 Kings. Deuteronomy is both the fifth book of the Pentateuch and also the first book of the DTR. Deuteronomy is actually a composite composition, pieced together from one set of material that is part of the Pentateuch and a second set of material that is part of the history of Israel and Judah that follows. Either way, the figure of Joshua finishes Israel's journey into the promised land, and I view the plot for the next block of material as being set forth in Joshua 23–24.

Epilogue

1. Although this book is mainly about the Old Testament narrative, I have mostly written about the psalms in my life as an Old Testament scholar. For an introduction to the psalms, see Rolf A. Jacobson and Karl N. Jacobson, *Invitation to the Psalms: A Reader's Guide for Discovery and Engagement* (Grand Rapids: Baker, 2013). For an in-depth commentary, see Nancy L. DeClaissé-Walford, Rolf A. Jacobson, and Beth LaNeel Tanner, *The Book of Psalms*, New International Commentary on the Old Testament (Grand Rapids: Eerdmans, 2014). I also have written on the psalms at Working Preacher and Enter the Bible, two Luther Seminary owned websites. I am sure that some of my themes repeat themselves and that I borrow from what I have written there. My earlier thoughts, plagiarized from myself, are used with the permission of the author and the permission of my publishers. Thank you.

2. This section borrows heavily from Rolf Jacobson, "My Favorite Bible Passage—Rolf Jacobson," Enter the Bible, April 1, 2015, https://tinyurl.com/ycg2gyum. Used with permission.